MORE
THAN A
RELIGION

DYING TO THE TRADITIONS OF MEN, COMING TO LIFE IN THE POWER OF GOD

C.J. Greiner

MORE THAN A RELIGION

Edited by Dylan Cruz

Cover Design by Manuel Gaitan

Printed by CreateSpace

Marketing/Editing by Emily Suxo

Printed in the United States of America

ISBN-10: 171735176X
ISBN-13: 978-1717351760

DEDICATION

To my beautiful wife.

Your persistence to love God no matter what happens in this life, drives me to live a life of reverence towards God more and more every day.

I am honored to spend the rest of my life with you.

I love you.

I also want to dedicate this book to anyone who has never been shown the truth of God's word. Or for those who have been living by tradition for years and have finally seen the Truth. You may think those years are lost, but I want you to know God is a redeemer of time. He can restore what has been taken from you.

MORE THAN A RELIGION

CONTENTS

MORE THAN A RELIGION

ACKNOWLEDGMENTS

I would like to thank a special group of people who made all this possible. Thank you to my mother who loves me with everything she has. Your support and love for me doesn't go unnoticed. I want to thank my father and step-mom (Larry and Ruby). Thank you for always loving Leana and I. Your joyful giving encourages us every day. Thank you to my wonderful mother-in-law, Irma Rivera (my Madre) and her constant support and encouragement. Special thanks to my father-in-law, Ramon Rivera. Your generosity is overwhelming and I thank you for your love and support. You show me what a real man of God is all about. Thank you to those who gave financially: Darleen Diaz, Dylan Cruz, Kevin Torio, Artie Lugo, April and Brian Huynh, and Miguel and Jessica Palmerin. I am so thankful for your generosity!

I want to thank Pastor Manuel and Aurora Santillano, you two have been like parents to us since we arrived to Harvest Time. Thank you for your countless hours you have poured into us and thank you for your faithfulness and obedience.

To Harvest Time Church, you guys are the best family anyone could ask for. We are honored to serve next to you. Your encouragement is absolutely amazing.

Thank you to Charlie Reynoso and Star Hardware for your generosity. I believe God will continue to prosper your business due to your love for Him and your honor and dedication to your employees.

To Mark and Peggy Driscoll, thank you! Your prayers and sacrifice throughout the years created such a strong foundation in all of us. I can honestly say Leana and I wouldn't be where we are today if it wasn't for you. Thank you for your obedience. I have never stopped using all you have taught us.

Big thanks to Rene Padron and his wife, Andrea. Thank you for your obedience, for speaking the truth with boldness, and calling my wife and I out to speak into our life. We are eternally grateful.

MORE THAN A RELIGION

FORWARD

It has been a great honor to get to know C.J. Greiner and his wife Leana. I was very excited to read this book that the Lord put on C.J.'s heart a while ago. As I read through the pages that you are about to dive into, I asked the Lord to open my heart, my mind, and my ears to His voice. I wanted to be open and completely surrendered to hear God's message through the book. I beckon you to be sensitive to the voice of the Lord and do the same. You will hear it through the following chapters.

C.J. has a true gift from the Lord that allows him to be completely raw and honest. The Holy Spirit has led him to still be encouraging in the same manner. C.J. has great knowledge of the scriptures and the ability to break it down where it is easy to understand and to challenge you to be in better fellowship with our savior Jesus. It was refreshing to read a book that comes from the heart of a man who has truly encountered Jesus and not just studied the word. It challenges the reader to draw closer to the Lord. This is the heart of Jesus, for people to come unto Him and continue to draw closer. I have read books by other Christian authors, but this book is set apart because it gives you a sneak peek into C.J.'s secret place and prayer life.

I grew up in a Christian home and have been saved and immersed in my relationship with the Lord for over 27 years. I loved reading this book that has challenged me and has made me search my heart. You can sense the anointing and the presence of God all over these pages. I believe this book has been written in God's perfect timing with what the Church is going through in our world today with an ordained purpose to challenge every believer all over the world.

I strongly encourage every believer, every minister, and ministry leader to read this book and make this book a part of those books we tend to read every year because of the reminders and revelations you will receive. I believe this book is going to impact every believer around the world into a deeper and loving relationship with Jesus Christ. I pray that as you turn the page that your prayer will be the same as mine: "Jesus speak to me through this book, let me hear your voice and challenge my heart and every area of my life. Amen."

-**RENE PADRON**, Evangelist
Miracles Happen Ministries
Co-Founder, CEO & President

"Reading through the first few chapters of this book, I am moved by the transparency and how relevant CJ's words are. It brings me great joy to know that God is raising up a generation of Firebrands in the earth who are passionate about getting serious with the presence of God— a generation that will stop making Him sit through our compromise. This book will not only mark you with a fresh passion to go deeper in your walk with God, but will speak to your core and shake every complacency in your life."

-**Matt Cruz**, Evangelist
Matt Cruz Ministries
Founder of the Rise Up Movement

More Than A Religion

INTRODUCTION

Dear friends,

I'm going to be honest with you. I have sat down many times in the past three years trying to write a new book. Every time I opened my laptop and began to type, I felt like something was not right. I have so much I want to say, so much I want to share, but I realized that nothing is worth sharing unless God prompts it on your heart to share. All of us could write a book if we really wanted to, but the real question isn't whether we CAN, it's whether we SHOULD. I have now come to the realization, that God didn't want me writing another book, at least not in that particular season. Could I have still written one? Sure! But would it be as influential? Probably not. Would it be as powerful? I don't think so. We are always asked, "What do YOU want to be or do in life?" But we are rarely asked, what does GOD wants us to be or do. His plans are greater, right?

Years ago as I began to write my first book, "#DearChristianMen," the Lord shared with me a word that would frame my entire life. He said to me, **A thousand words from man, cannot compare to the power of one word from Me--God.** In other words, we can preach so many great sermons and do so many awesome things on our own strength and maybe it would impact a little, but they will never compare and never influence as much as if God was the one orchestrating those words through you. To simplify it even more, I didn't want to write a single book, a single blog, a single status unless God told me to-- because when God tells you to do something, He is going to back you up and that gives you the assurance to know, it's for a powerful purpose. If God says "Lay hands on that sick person," you have to know He is going to heal them or else He wouldn't have told you to lay hands on them.

Same thing applies with a book. If God said, "Write this book," you better believe it's for a greater reason beyond yourself. So when I got the green light to write this book I was ecstatic! Because I love the attention and money? No way! It's because I know He wants to use me to touch, heal, save, and deliver others! That's why I do this. That's why I share, write, and blog. The feeling you get when someone reads your book and it completely changes the way they see God and others, it's more rewarding than any amount of money.

The biggest question right now, is why did I write this book? The answer is simple: to ignite a fire within the Church and see a generation exemplify a life of truly living for God with all their hearts—no longer viewing a relationship with God as casual and something to be taken lightly. We as the American Church have taken mindsets and lifestyles that other men and women have taught over the years, and we have ran with them, never really praying or studying whether or not they were even biblical! We have based our entire Christianity off of our own personal experiences or inexperience, bringing the Word of God down to our lifestyles instead of rising up and transforming our minds and way of living to imitate Christ! Let's be honest with ourselves here, we have lived off the revelation of men and women more than our own revelation of God, and in doing so, we have infused ourselves with the traditions of men, creating a generation of believers who are just like the Pharisees. The religious leaders literally ignored the commands of God, just so they could hold on to their human traditions. Being a Christian is more than a religion of do's and don'ts, it is developing a relationship with Jesus Christ, and coming to know His character and will through the Holy Scripture, not tradition or popular belief.

My old pastor back in Iowa used to tell us before every service, "*No matter what I say, what I preach, or what I teach, study it out, read your Bible and find out if I am telling the Truth. I am a man, sometimes I miss it. If I say something that does not line up with the Word of God, throw it out!*" This was embedded into my brain, but it has blessed me more than ever. So now, no matter who it is, it could even be my wife, if it does not line up with scripture, it's not worth keeping. But this very concept has been ignored throughout the years as we have just taken other's word for it.

I have come to realize that we tend to live by tradition a lot more than we realize. Tradition can easily become culture. If you were raised in a home with parents that constantly worried and was always in fear, their tradition could easily become your culture. It increases your chance of taking on that tradition of fear and becoming a person who has anxiety. The tradition of lukewarm and casual Christianity has been passed down from generation to generation, mainly be example. Have you heard of the Rule of First Mention? Whatever we are taught first about a subject, that will become our base of comparison. For example, if we were taught that God can't be reached on an intimate level, then, when someone comes along and tells us that God wants relationship with us, we will weigh what we just heard (truth) and compare it to our foundation (tradition), always leaning more towards our first mention, rather than weighing tradition against Truth.

Men and women, I am writing this book so that your eyes may be opened to false mindsets about God or casual lifestyles that we may have picked up on over the years, through tradition. My goal is for a people of God to rise up, die to the traditions of men, and come to life in the power of God! I want to see a generation not afraid to get uncomfortable because, let's be honest, God's word is uncomfortable! I want to see a group of believers that imitate Jesus and His ministry, that love beyond what they "think" love is, rather are led more by the Spirit than they are their emotions. I want to see Christians who are not just talking with wise and persuasive words, but literally walking in the demonstration of the power of the Spirit! I pray we will rise up and step out of this lukewarm, casual living for God, and understand that God is looking for a people of faith, whose hearts are fully for him!

Before you start the first chapter I want you to do something. Pray right now that God opens your eyes and opens your ears to the things that He wants you to know. And, like my old pastor taught me, if you see anything that may not line up with scripture or maybe it's a little off, research it, study it out and find out for yourself if it is truth or of man. I love you guys and I thank you for choosing this book. May it bless you and deepen your relationship with the Father.

> *"These are the wise sayings of Solomon,*
> *David's son, Israel's king—*
> *Written down so we'll know how to live well and right,*
> *to understand what life means and where it's going;*
> *A manual for living,*
> *for learning what's right and just and fair;*
> *To teach the inexperienced the ropes*
> *and give our young people a grasp on reality.*
> *There's something here also for seasoned men and women,*
> *still a thing or two for the experienced to learn—*
> *Fresh wisdom to probe and penetrate,*
> *the rhymes and reasons of wise men and women.*
> *Start with God—the first step in learning is bowing down*
> *to God;*

only fools thumb their noses at such wisdom and learning."
-Proverbs 1:1-7 (MSG)

ONE

Intro

As a teenager I had been going to church and youth group since I was in 7th grade. That was awesome, the only problem was that I never made an effort to read the Bible. It was gibberish to me and not a single Christian's lifestyle ever made me desire to. I never got my definition of love from the Word, just how Christians acted and how the world displayed it. I remember one time some kids had messed with my friend and I and made us mad. My friend wanted to plot revenge on them but, I had my doubts of whether or not we should. I remember our pastor talking about loving our neighbors and even our enemies, which I wasn't even fully sure what that looked like, but as I explained it to my friend, he interrupted me with, *"Yea, but the Bible also says, 'an eye for an eye and tooth for tooth.'"* He had been a Christian all his life so, who was I to argue? So I went with it. In that moment, revenge became normal for me because I thought it was biblical.

Years down the road, after I had truly gotten saved and dedicated my entire life to Jesus, I remember studying the Bible about love and had come across this very scripture in **Matthew 5:38**, "*You have heard that it was said, 'Eye for eye, and tooth for tooth*.' But Jesus was quoting this in order to say this immediately after, *"But I tell you, do not resist an evil person. If anyone slaps you on the right cheek, turn to them the other cheek also* (**Matthew 5:38**)." And even in verse 43 it says, *"You have heard that it was said, 'Love your neighbor and hate your enemy.' But I tell you, love your enemies and pray for those who persecute you, that you may be children of your Father in heaven..."*

For a long time, I had believed the traditions of man when it came to what love truly was. Instead of knowing what God said about the matter, I searched it out through internet, TV shows, and even relationships in the world. I never realized it but my perception of love was molded and shaped by tradition, which is where many Christians are today. We tend to pick and choose how to love and who to love. In this chapter, I press in on some areas that we all can be better at, and even some areas that may be hard to swallow. It's time we die to the traditions of tolerance and come to life in the power of real love.

In my last book I had a chapter called, *"God Loves You,"* and I went into detail of how much God truly loves you. Now, it's so hard to cover the subject of love within one chapter because there is so much depth to love, due to the fact that God IS love. In the past three years my understanding of love has grown exponentially, which is why I am adding a chapter in this book, as well. You can never talk too much about love. In fact, in this chapter I don't want to just talk about what love is, I want to talk about what it's not, as well as false mindsets that our culture and tradition has embedded in us about what love is.

It's crazy how love is the foundation of the entire Bible, yet we tend to forget that's the reason why we are saved and why we do what we do. We tend to justify our love for others by saying things like, "*I love them, BUT...,*" or, "*I know I need to love them, BUT....*" Here's the deal, anytime you say "but" you are changing the whole dynamic of what you just said. I really want to write a book called, "*The Big Buts of The Bible,*" because Paul does this a lot. He says one thing but then shifts the whole idea of the topic by adding a "*but.*" That's actually another subject I will talk about but, I'll save it for another section. Here's the thing, the more we understand what love is, the more we see what it isn't, we then start to see ourselves in the light of love, as well as others around us. The more we understand love, the better we will understand our purpose.

Putting Love in a box

There are times in our life when we have such a small concept of love. Sometimes our understanding of love is but through a peep hole. Who says love can't be loud and bold? Who says love doesn't correct, rebuke, or exhort? "*Preach the word; be prepared in season and out of season; correct, rebuke and encourage—with great patience and careful instruction* (**2 Timothy 4:2**)." Love is gentle, yes, but sometimes it requires our voices to rise, it requires us to shout, as if someone close to us was sleep walking towards a cliff. New age religion and thinking, is teaching us that those who are passionate and loud are judgmental and mean. Honestly, sometimes we have to step out of the box and try to find love in all faucets.

Most of you may have heard about an evangelist/revivalist by the name of Isaiah Saldivar. If you know him, then you know his delivery of the word of God can be very bold and very loud. The first time I had listened to him, I remember turning to my friend in the car ride home and saying, *"He is right, but why does he have to yell?"* I began to pick apart his delivery method. I tried to find as many flaws as I could to his message, just so I would feel less convicted. I came to a conclusion: Yes, sometimes we need a shake, and yes, the gospel can be delivered in a gentle way, and I realized that Isaiah's method may not be ideal to most Christians, but it was still truth, and sometimes the truth has to be delivered in a way that will shake foundations. (side note: no matter how the message is delivered, love should always be the foundation of it. We must be careful we do not preach from a position of hurt or anger, but the Holy Spirit at all times.)

When you wake someone up, you make sure they can hear you. When there is danger up ahead, there is an urgency and a passion to warn. The reason why I was getting upset was because I knew he was right. I knew what he was saying was truth. My spirit was craving for me to take the correction, but my flesh wanted me to become judgmental and critical towards him, giving myself an excuse not to listen to him. What happens when our own sin is exposed? We point out someone else's flaws, because if we can find them guilty of something, it takes the pressure off us! The way he delivered that message that night was a new style of preaching to me, which made me very quick to judge it as "condemning" and "unlovely." At that moment, I began to put love in a box, as if love could not be loud and bold. In the state the American church is in, I say we could use a good shaking from God and those sent by Him.

It's true though, we all tend to put love into our own little, man-made idea of what it really is and how it should be delivered. We tend to define love very vaguely. We have this notion that love is always this happy-go-lucky, rainbows and butterflies, gentle, hippy love. Like Jesus calmly came and accepted and tolerated everything and everyone and if anyone was loud, bold, or corrected anyone, then they were violating the law of love. Nope, sorry, didn't happen like that. In fact, Jesus was very in-your-face and definitely did not hold back at times.

We must understand this; everything Jesus did was love. In fact, He WAS love because, He was God and the exact representation of His being (**Hebrews 1:3**). Jesus was God manifested in human form, and Jesus only ever did what He saw the Father do and only ever said what He heard the Father say (**John 5:19; John 12:49; John 7:16**). So we can clearly see by scripture that everything Jesus did and said was completely out of love, plus the fact that he never sinned (**1 Peter 2:22; 2 Corinthians 5:21**). So we can agree that every word and every action Jesus did was perfectly without sin, right?

If you have read the Gospels, then you have a good understanding that Jesus wasn't always a gentle preacher. Actually, there was some times where He spoke in such a way that many churches would probably have kicked Him out. An example of His gentleness could be seen in **John 8:1-11**. This is the story of the woman caught in adultery. The religious leaders drug her out and threw her before Jesus and mentioned that the Law stated that someone caught in adultery should rightfully be stoned. Jesus then said something that would change the entire message of God, *"He who is without sin among you, let him throw a stone at her first,"* (**John 8:7 NJKV**). One by one the religious leaders dropped their stones and left. Jesus looked at the woman and asked her, *"Woman, where are those accusers of yours? Has no one condemned you?"* The woman replied, *"No one, Lord."* Jesus responds, *"Neither do I condemn you; go and sin no more,"* (**John 8:11 NKJV**)

This whole passage overflows with love. Jesus was completely gentle with this woman and I am pretty sure no one will argue that this was completely out of love, right? But then you have the many times Jesus was bold and loud to the religious leaders. Or what about the time Jesus called the religious leaders a, *"brood of vipers,"* or in other words, *"you snakes*!" (**Matthew 12:34 NIV**)? Or the time Jesus flipped over tables and drove off the money changers out of the temple with a whip (**Mark 11:15-17: John 2:15**). If someone did this here in the American church, Christians would be trying to cast a devil out of Him. Actually, they would probably say something like, *"That's not what Jesus would do. Who are you to judge? That's not love, just pray for them."* Jesus and His message of repentance would probably not be very popular now days.

You might look at that and think, *"That's not very nice,"*

but the thing is, everything that Jesus did was out of love. Contrary to popular belief, Jesus loved the religious leaders. He loved them so much, he HAD to tell them the truth. We tend to look at love through a very small hole, but what I love about the Bible and Jesus' ministry is that He shows us the huge spectrum of love. We see the side of love that is gentle, caring, and quiet, but then we see the side of love that is rough, bold, and loud!

When something happens that doesn't fit our little idea of love, we look down on it as though it's from the devil. We have created a bad habit of always receiving rough, bold, and loud things as condemnation. Many Christians have what I like to call, *an ear of condemnation*. So whenever someone preaches a loud, fiery message that is unfamiliar with us, we process it as mean, offensive, and condemning, so we turn our ears and eyes away from truth, away from the message that could truly set us free.

Don't get me wrong, there are people out there who do preach loud and bold messages that are from a condemning heart, but even if it is, I honestly believe we can still take at least one thing away from that teaching—but do not be quick to throw a message away. The point of all this is to expand your definition of love, because with such a small idea of what love is, we can lose out on receiving everything God has for us. I am not saying that every message should be loud, over and over again, striking the sheep. No, please hear me out, there is a time and a place. I am trying to prepare our hearts to not be moved so easily, and to have a better understanding that love can touch us in many faucets and many colors, which includes a message that is hard to swallow.

Whenever I go up to preach a message, I always want to just talk about God's promises and how He wants to give us the best. This is true, but there is a time and a place for that. When I desire to preach a message, many times I get different messages but with the same subject: *"Wake up, Church!"* I get loud, I get bold, and I can get intense. I get passionate because I look around and I see Christians playing church. I see them flipping the Jesus Switch and getting their happy, God-bless-you faces on, but then they go home, get on Facebook, and complain and post, like, and share worldly things. I hear them talk like the world, act like the world, and think like the world. Seeing all of this deeply saddens me because, I see the potential they could be living. I see all the great plans God has for them and yet, they are choosing short-term fulfillment, rather than eternal life. I see the healing that is waiting for them, I see deliverance from the pain and torture. I see a beautiful life they can have and yet, they choose the world and say things like, *"I believe in God. I love Jesus."*

This is why I preach how I preach, because I have an urgency; a grieving in my heart. *"The true man of God is heartsick, grieved at the worldliness of the Church, grieved at the toleration of sin in the Church, grieved at the prayerlessness in the Church. He is disturbed that the corporate prayer of the Church no longer pulls down the strongholds of the devil."* Leonard Ravenhill said this, and this is how I feel many times. Jesus did not come to deliver a feel-good, everything-is-alright message. He came with the message of repentance, rooted in love. A message that was real and raw, that pierced the very soul of those who listened. A message that offended people and made some angry (mostly those who already claimed to know God but didn't). Whether they were new or veterans in the faith, He preached the deep, hard-to-swallow truth. And those who didn't like it chose to walk away, but those who desired more, came to Him and were filled. I believe Jesus was grieved at the state of His Father's creation. There were times when He was so astonished and amazed at their lack of faith and sin, which is why He came and said what He said and did what He did, because He loved us with a bold, passionate love.

I remember a time when I was young and my parents were fighting. I remember them yelling at each other. I praise the Lord they are both saved now but, there was a time when their fighting was reckless. I tried to stop them, but my voice was drowned out by the yelling. It was then I screamed at the top of my lungs, *"Would you guys just stop!?"* They both got quiet and looked at me. It is then that they realized what they were doing and how they were acting. Sometimes, people need a bold shout in their life before they can actually see what they are doing wrong. You have to remember one thing; the devil is shouting lies into people's minds daily and sometimes, in order for them to hear past those lies, you may need to deliver a bold and loud message that shakes their foundation and makes them uncomfortable.

It's time we expand our understanding of love. Instead of fitting love in the mold of our mind, we need to expand our mind around the full spectrum of love.

Real discipline is real love

I remember watching this news broadcast one night in San Antonia, TX, where they were talking about this little girl that calls herself, "Lil Tay." I had never heard of her but I guess she is this nine-year-old girl that has 2.1 million followers on Instagram. She makes these videos where she is in nice cars and throws around cash, all while saying explicit and derogatory remarks. Let's just say I was starting to get over my post-flight headache but listening to her made it come back. That's not even the worse part. What really saddened me was that her mother fully supported her lifestyle.

They were interviewing the mother and Lil Tay together; the reporter was asking them a series of questions where her mother explained how the happiness of her daughter is the most important thing to her, and this is what makes her daughter happy. At this point my mind is melting into a bowl of soup. As sad as it truly was, I could see a resemblance of American Christianity in there. We have either been taught or we have convinced ourselves that this is how love looks, that God just wants us to be happy, therefore we can do what we want. There is a bit of hyper-grace mixed in with ignorance, with a teaspoon of pure evil in this mindset. But it's a reality for so many, which leads them to fully believe, this is what love is. Deep down I saw the pain and emptiness in this mother's eyes. In fact, she stopped being a mother at this point and became an enabler for her daughter, because if you truly loved your daughter you would discipline her and tell her how to truly act, even if it makes her feel angry or unhappy in that moment, knowing that someday, when she is living a morally sound life, she is going to thank you. *"There is a way that seems right to a man but in the end it leads to death,"* **Proverbs 14:12**. And that's just it; unsubmitted emotions, and our flesh, will lead us into a life that seems like life, it feels like love, and it looks like happiness, but it will only lead us to death and destruction.

Dr. Jonathan Welton writes in his book, "New Covenant Revolution," *"A lot of people have definitions of love that do not align with God's nature. Like the Antinomians of old, they want to believe that love means there is no law, and true love embraces every person and action without reproof. They believe sin is an old covenant word, and as a result, they define love as something that is permissive rather than liberating. In other words, it removes the idea of sin instead of empowering us to overcome sin. The Bible teaches us something different."* And there it is, the sad truth. There is this false love going around, infecting the churches across America, convincing people that real love is tolerant, all-accepting, and without correction. This mother is convinced that if she lets her child do what she wants, she is loving her, but in fact, she isn't truly loving her child if she doesn't ever TEACH her and WARN her about the effect this life will have on her. Nowhere in the Bible will you find Jesus tolerating sin, and nowhere in the Bible will you find people coming to Jesus as they are, but staying there the same. God will embrace you the way you are, but loves you enough to not let you stay there. The Bible says in **Hebrews 12:8**, *"If you are not disciplined (and everyone undergoes discipline), then you are illegitimate children and not true sons. Moreover, we have* *all had human fathers who discipline us and we respected them for it. How much more should we submit to the Father of our spirits and live! Our fathers disciplined us for a little while as they thought best; but God disciplines us for our good, that we may share in his holiness. No discipline seems pleasant at the time, but painful. Later on, however, it produces a harvest of righteousness and peace for those who have been trained by it."*

Although discipline is never fun, it's always worth it in the end. I remember my grandma would always tell me to turn the light off when I leave the room, or she would tell me to quit running the water if I didn't need it. I always thought she was just nagging at me. Like, what's the big deal? As I begin to live on my own and I got my first electric; and water bill, I thought I was going to have a heart-attack. After all those years of her both teaching me and reprimanding me, I finally realized why she did it; shortly later, I found myself turning off the lights and using only a little bit of water, when necessary.

This Lil Tay may not like it if she gets disciplined, but I guarantee you she will thank her mother one day when she is living a righteous and peaceful life. Parents and future parents, if you are reading this, be a parent, not a friend to your children. It doesn't mean you can't be nice and hangout with them, but when it comes down to it, children need a parent who truly loves them and will tell them the unadulterated truth. Your job is not to bring your kids a happiness that THEY think is happiness, your job is to do what is right, train them up in the ways of God, discipline them when needed, and watch them grow into men and women of God and experience true freedom and real joy.

One thing this little girl said that really got me thinking was when the reporter asked about her cursing and using profanity in her videos, Lil Tay responded, "*I don't really do that stuff in real life, just in the videos.*" I shouted at the Television, "*That is real life! Everything you are doing is in real life!*" But isn't this how so many of us have lived or is still living now? We put on our nice clothes and our smiles as we go to church, we talk properly and use Christianese slang, lift our hands and say amen, but once we leave those four walls, our entire manner changes. We are just as blinded as this little girl is. We think that just because we are "good" in church, that it's ok to watch and listen to certain music outside of church. Some of us even think that just because we have a calling on our life, that we can do what we want and still lead in the church. God is calling you out of that lie, he is desiring a people who live holy inside the four walls of the church building, in addition to those whom live the exact same way when we leave. He is desiring us to heave pure hearts, free from moral corruption, free from certain music and certain shows. God is desiring us to be set a part, especially in our secret place when no one is watching! Real life is both inside the church AND outside the church! It is when the world is watching, as well as when no one sees you.

Extreme living equals extreme results

My wife reminded me that a lot of those Christians who are living holy, are the ones being persecuted by "Christians," calling them, *"Too much,"* or, *"Overly spiritual."* I want to encourage you, do not let the persecution of non-Christians or even Christians, discourage you from living a holy life for God. Do not be afraid to speak the truth and offend. We cannot water down the word to satisfy itching ears. **2 Timothy 4:4**, *"Preach the Word; be prepared in season and out of season; correct, rebuke and encourage-with great patience and careful instruction. <u>For the time will come when men will not put up with sound doctrine. Instead, to suit their own desires, they will gather around them a great number of teachers to say what their itching ears want to hear. They will turn their ears away from the truth and turn aside to myths</u>."*

There was a time my wife and I were looked at and called, *"Judgmental,"* or, *"Too spiritual,"* because we preached and lived out the uncompromising truth of the gospel. We were not afraid to correct people and stand up for holiness. We knew the importance of being careful of what kind of music we listen to and what kind of movies we watch. We didn't listen to popular secular artists, nor supported certain famous people, no matter how giving, popular, or talented they were. We didn't jump on any bandwagons, neither did we give a foothold in our lives for the enemy. Were we perfect? Of course not, but we tried our hardest to be careful of what we let in our lives. Yea, people said things and minute remarks were made, Christians looked at us funny, but do you think that Jesus, on Judgment Day, will say to me, *"CJ, you took me to seriously!"*?

I'm not trying to brag but, we were the real deal. We weren't putting on a show or trying to impress anyone. We just wanted to please God and love people back to life. Extreme living causes extreme results. Although there may be some resistance, in the end, we knew deep down that we had a job to love people; to love them so much that we were not willing to tolerate sin in our lives. We loved them so much that we were not willing to address the issues that were holding people back from living in the fullness of Christ.

Tolerance is not love. In fact, I believe if we tolerate and accept sin in our Churches, we are just as guilty as the ones who commit it. There can be no room for sin, and tolerating and accepting sinful lifestyles in fear of offending is such a problem in our Churches today. John Scott says this about tolerance and legalism, "*Tolerance is not a spiritual gift; it is the distinguishing mark of postmodernism; and sadly, it has permeated the very fiber of Christianity. Why is it that those who have no biblical convictions or theology to govern and direct their actions are tolerated and the standard or truth of God's Word rightly divided and applied is dismissed as extreme opinion or legalism?*"

Tolerance is often championed by people who have no foundation, and truly have nothing to stand for. G.K. Chesterton even says, "*Tolerance is the virtue of the man without convictions.*" Now, I am not saying we dishonor people who don't agree with us or choose to live differently, but we cannot walk by in this life unfazed by the sin and corruption of others, especially the Body of Christ; the ones who are called by God himself to find our lives in Him, and take on His characteristics of holiness and sanctification.

If you were to ask my, "*How do I get to Los Angeles?*" and I responded, "*Oh, just take any road you desire and they all will lead you there,*" you would question my sanity and you would doubt my truthfulness. The road to the Father is narrow, yet so many Christians have been convinced that the pathway to Heaven is large enough to take them and all their sins they keep holding onto and indulging in.

In fact, Jesus was so intolerant of our lost state, that He left His throne in the heavens, took on the form of a man, suffered at the hands of His creation, and died the cruelest death known to man, just to purchase our freedom from that very sin that we partake in. He couldn't look down on sin lightly, and He could not be broad-minded about his creation who was bound by it's desires. This was the reason He was so hard on the Pharisees, who outwardly looked good, but inwardly were dirty (**Matthew 23:25**). He was tolerant towards the sinner, He loved them, but intolerant toward the sin that enslaved them. That's why he didn't condemn the woman caught in adultery, but still addressed her sin saying, "Go and sin no more," (**John 8:11**). He loved her but absolutely hated the sin she was in. I feel like every Christian's slogan should be **1 Corinthians 15:34**, "*Awake to righteousness, and do not sin.*" Or even **Isaiah 1:16**, "*Wash yourselves, make yourselves clean; put away the evil of your doings from before My eyes. Cease to do evil...*"

The cross was God's evidence that He was so far from a tolerant God, in fact, it shows us the seriousness of how we should handle sin. Jesus was nailed to that cross that said, "*I love you, I do not condemn you, but go and sin no more*"

TWO

THE CRITICAL SPIRIT

Intro

One thing I have learned over the years is that when you begin to learn who you truly are in Christ, and what powers await for you in the name of Jesus, the enemy always tries to creep in and fill us up with pride to the point that we can become critical of others, critical of God, and even critical of ourselves, without even realizing it. There was a point I felt entitled because I was "filled with the Holy Spirit," and without realizing, I tried disguising it with confidence in Christ. There has been this tradition that has crept into the church and it causes division among denominations. There is this tradition that says to stay away from any Christian who doesn't believe exactly what you believe, or that, just because we have differences, we cannot unite. And over time, we embraced it and it became a part of our Christian life.

I will be honest with you, I looked at other Christians who were not baptized in the Spirit as if they didn't truly love or know God, and the day that my eyes were opened to God's grace and mercy, I wept like a child. How could I have looked at my fellow brothers and sisters like that? How could I look at someone and know their entire life and their heart? We are all on different levels and we are all in different battles, but no matter what, we are all the body of Christ. I thought to myself, "*It's time to go back to the heart of worship: JESUS CHRIST.*"

In this chapter I try to break a lot of strongholds that tradition has taught us about God, about others, and even about ourselves. It's time we die to the critical spirit and come to life in the power of Grace and Truth.

*"One of the most difficult defilements of the spirit to deal with is the critical spirit. A critical spirit has its roots in pride. Because of the 'plank' of pride in our own eye we are not capable of dealing with the 'speck' of need in someone else. We are often like the Pharisee who, completely unconscious of his own need prayed "God, I thank you that I am not like the other men" (**Luke 18:11**). We are quick to see—and to speak of—the faults of others, but slow to see our own needs. How sweetly we relish the opportunity to speak critically of someone else—even when we are unsure of the facts. We forget that "a man who stirs up dissension among brothers" by criticizing one to another is one of the "six things which the Lord hates"* (Proverbs 6:16-19)" -Jerry bridges

Social Media: Our critical platform

One of the worst things you can do as a Christian is scroll through the comment section of a Christian post, article, or video. It shouldn't be, but it is. It's a sad truth that has become the norm for social media: Nobody is laying hands on the sick and praying for the lost, but behind the computer screen, people have become bold scholars and theologians. I am going to go a step further and add the word, "Critical," to the list.

Insecurity and jealousy has been the cause of so many Christians having a critical spirit towards others. Focusing on man and not the Lord can cause one to be critical of every flaw of others. We have to remember that Satan is the *"accuser of the brethren,"* (**Revelation 12:10**) and sadly can work through or influence us as believers, to accomplish his work of tearing people down. Those who are fault-finders and constant critics of people and situations, are usually sick in the body, fearful, and stressed out. The solution to this lies in scripture, *"Stop passing judgment on one another."* We must begin to love others in the body of Christ, uplifting them, edifying them, correcting when you have to, and building them up in love.

Social media has opened a huge door for Christians to be some of the most critical people, on the planet. Everyone seems to think the world needs their two cents on every topic, and if we are being truly honest here, because I believe in complete transparency, I have been this type of Christian many times before. I was afraid to preach the gospel in public for fear of rejection, but I was a master theologian behind the computer screen—leaving critical comments and debating people left and right. I thought I was doing God a favor by doing this, but no one truly leaves comments with a heart to receive correction, which is why it's a complete waste of time to even attempt to debate people on a subject over the internet.

This issue goes beyond the internet and into the churches as well. We have become critical of pastors, worship leaders, evangelists, prophets, apostles, just about any position in the Body of Christ. We have taken on a critical spirit and crucified people with our words. I will be bold here and say this: when we do this we are so un-Christ like, it's devilish. Yup, it's of the devil when we are critical towards others, especially leaders! I am not saying you are possessed by a demon, I am saying you are being influenced more by the enemy in this area than God. The real question is this: Do you want to rid yourself of a critical spirit? Do you always find yourself being negative or jealous towards others? Do you feel like you are the faith party-pooper, always expecting the worse, even after you prayed for restoration? When others are promoted around you, do you rejoice with them or think to yourself that you deserved that promotion? These are all signs of a critical spirit and if you can't first identify these symptoms, put your pride down and humble yourself under correction, or it could manifest into something worse. Sooner or later, you will reap what you sow.

In May of 2018, our Church had put on a 4-day revival conference in Covina, CA. It was an amazing and powerful weekend. On the third night, a bunch of us went to In-N-Out after the service. It had to have been 11 0'clock at night, and about 30 of us were all sitting together on one side of the restaurant when all of the sudden, one of our leaders started singing, "*Reckless Love,*" by Cory Asbury. The rest of our group started joining in and before we knew it, we sang the whole song right there at In-N-out, for everyone to hear. The thing is, we didn't do it for attention or to show everyone we are Christians. We all were so full of God and so excited about all He had been doing at this conference, that it just happened.

Without anyone really knowing, Marcus Rogers began to record our singing and uploaded it to his social media. Within days it had around 300,000 views and CBN, the 700 Club, and a couple other Christian broadcasting pages started talking about it and posting the video. It was awesome to see, but of course, you will always have those people who are critical towards everything. I started scrolling through the comments one day and started to see so many people saying things like, *"They are just doing this for the views,"* and even stuff like, *"If they really were worshiping God, they wouldn't have recorded it."* Yea, it was so petty and so critical. These people had no idea who we were or what we were about. I just remember David dancing carelessly for the Lord, looking like a fool, but he did not care, God was the only thing on his mind. David's wife, on the other hand, thought he was a fool. She despised him in her heart, mocking his behavior, *"How the king of Israel has distinguished himself today, going around half-naked in full view of the slave girls of his servants as any vulgar fellow would!"* But David replied, *"Yes, and I am willing to look even more foolish than this, even to be humiliated in my own eyes! But those servant girls you mentioned will indeed think I am distinguished!"* **(2 Samuel 6:20-22 NLT)** David was a man after God's heart, being embarrassed or being labelled as a fool was not even on his mind, he just wanted to honor God and worship Him. His wife mocked him for being set apart, but David embraced it, having no fear of what man will say.

If anyone knows our church, then they know we have some of the most genuine, passionate, in-love-with-God people around. Stuff like this happens more often with our church, than most people think. And it's not for attention, it's just an overflow of the love our people have for God. So, of course, people just looked at the surface of the situation and started assuming things. It really irritated me as I was reading these comments, but just then God gave me flashbacks of the times that I was critical, just like these people. I saw times where I was critical towards Christians for having money, and it was only in the times that I myself was being greedy with my money, and I was in lack because of it. I saw times that I was critical towards people posting videos of them praying for other people or blessing people, and it was only during the times in my life when I was being lazy—never stepping out and laying hands on the sick or praying for the broken and lost. He asked me, "*Do you see a pattern?*" I realized that I was critical towards others in the areas of my life that I was lacking in. And it convicted me because, I was ready to fire back at some of these people and set them straight, but then I would have become just like them. I don't fully know another man's heart, so I can't say exactly why these people were critical, but you can get a glimpse of it by the words they speak and how they say it.

Critical and narrow-minded

In response to this, I have been asked a handful of times on what I think about the song, *"Reckless Love,"* by Cory Asbury, and I try not to have an "opinion" too much on such widely debated topics, but I try to understand things by biblical text, because let's face it, that's what really matter right? I encourage you to watch Cory Asbury's video on him explaining the meaning behind it, because if you don't, you can easily get all uptight and critical about the word "reckless." Yes, it's a word used mostly to negatively describe something or a situation, BUT let's look deeper into the heart behind it.

There are strong points on both ends, but the biggest thing we tend to do when we look at this song is take it literal. This is for the critical, opinionated Christians out there. The entire Bible is not literal, in fact, Paul used some "creative" words in **1 Corinthians 1:25**, *"For the foolishness of God is wiser than human wisdom, and the weakness of God is stronger than human strength."* First glance and many Christians would yell, *"blasphemy,"* and start melting in their seats. Paul isn't calling God foolish, because we all know there is no foolishness in God and there is no weakness in Him. Deep down, he isn't calling the gospel or anything related to God actually foolish. Paul literally gave his entire life to preaching the gospel. When Paul says this, is he making timeless—universal theological assertions? Is he saying that foolishness is objectively a divine characteristic of the Father? Is he saying that God is actually weak? No. He's getting creative with language; Paul took words with a conventionally negative connotation and subverted those cultural associations by using them in a different way in order to pass on an understanding of God and the Gospel.

So what do I say about this? Quit over-thinking things, quit being critical, watch your words, but also look at the heart of a song or situation. Petty things like this is what is dividing the body of Christ, and until we can learn to look past these things and reverence God together as a body, then we will never see true unity. Pick your religious wedgie and keep moving forward.

Self-evaluate

As I began to be vulnerable about this situation, my good friend, Daniel Zimbler, shared my post and wrote these wise words, "*I've been thinking about this sort of thing a lot lately. The things that get on my nerves or make me 'opinionated," Am I that way because they are wrong or because I'm not seeing them in my life, so my jealousy is putting a selfish wall up to 'protect' my feelings when in actuality it's dragging me down and taking me out of my anointing. Self-evaluation is something God has really been growing me in. I want to be able to see these things in my life before someone has to pull me aside and confront it.*" I wanted to repost his repost right there because that was such a true word.

We look at people and their promotions or their fruit and we get jealous because we are not seeing those types of results in our own lives, so instead of putting our pride down and striving to be better and go deeper, we get offended, put up a wall, go on defense, and strike back with a critical spirit. How many of us can honestly say we rejoice with those who rejoice? Let's be honest here, how many of us have watched people around you get promoted and thought, "*I am so happy for them. That is so awesome*," without thinking that you should have been promoted too?

My pastor was talking with me the other day and said that he likes to watch people during times that they are not being used to see how they respond. Anyone can be happy while being used by the pastor, but how are you acting when pastor or leadership isn't calling on you? Those are true times of testing.

The dangerous truth is that we have a lot of critical Christians in the Church, and it all stems from a generation of participation trophy men and women who think that they deserve a certain position without hard work. We opened the door wide for jealousy and pride to come in and run our churches, run our families, and run our lives. **James 3:16** says, "*For where there is jealousy and selfish ambition, there you will find disorder and evil of every kind.*" This is Bible. This is no exaggeration. When we let jealousy and selfish ambition into our ways of thinking and living, we are literally inviting hell into our lives. Many Christians are trying to live a life for Christ, all while holding on to jealousy and bitterness, and they wonder why they are not seeing breakthrough; why their lives are still total messes. It's because you have opened the door for the enemy to come in and he is bringing all his pals with him.

The self-righteous Christian

If there is one thing I have been guilty of as a Christian, it was actually thinking I was better than some people because their sin was worse than mine. Can I be honest with you all? In those moments of judgement, I forgot all the sins and dirty secrets I used to live by, and the only thing I could see was the mistakes of everyone else. God forgave us and cleansed us, looking on us with grace and mercy, yet sometimes we look at others, and if we are truly honest with ourselves, we think of ourselves as a little higher than them, even if it's just a tiny bit. I have never saw the nastiness and the anger of some Christians until social media came out and Donald Trump became president. Christians trash talking him, calling him every name in the book, and to be honest, it reminded me of how I was at times, only I did it in a way where it looked like I was preaching, but in fact, my target was everyone except myself.

I was driving the other day to work, and I turned on my signal to get in the "exit only" lane. Out of nowhere this vehicle speeds up behind me, and lays on his horn. I quickly went back into my lane and raised my hand to apologize. As he drove by he gave me the middle finger. I was slightly annoyed. I then got right behind him and we both began to exit the freeway. The man, all of a sudden, swerved out of the exit lane, across the shoulder, and cut right in front of someone, back on the freeway. I am assuming he didn't realize it was an exit lane. As I drove by I looked at him and just shook my head. I was so frustrated I just wanted to yell, "HYPOCRITE!" As annoying as that was, it reminded me of how we all can be at times, whether we have just gotten saved, or we have been at this for a while. We get upset and frustrated at people's sins and mess-ups, yet, if we really look at the big picture, we are most likely guilty of the exact same thing. It's crazy how we can so easily see and remember other people's mess-ups, but forget our own failures, like God's forgiveness and mercy only goes so far. Let me tell you right now, your sin is just as bad as any sin. Sin is sin, and if we were to lay out all of our mess-ups and dirty secrets on the table for the world to see, you would be shutting your mouth pretty fast. It's the same way with any person that is in the spotlight. All eyes are on them, which makes it so easy for any failures to be exposed and blown up all over the internet. It's definitely easy to look and think, "*Man, they are messed up!*" We have to remember that Christ forgave us of a multitude of sins, even when we were His enemies. We don't decide who deserves forgiveness or not. That's not our job! And the moment we start viewing ourselves as better than someone else, is the moment we need just as much grace and mercy as that person.

I am not trying to justify anyone's sin. In fact, people need to be reminded of what sin does, plus, as you grow closer to Christ, the amount of sin in your life should be decreasing. I am trying to change prospective here of how we respond to and love people, because social media has caused an outbreak of Christians hiding behind their screens and trashing other churches, other Christians, and anybody who thinks differently than them. Now, the Bible does tell us to judge the fruit of someone's life (**Matthew 7:15-20**), but that doesn't mean you talk trash about them in a condemning way.

Matthew 7: 1-5 says, *"Do not judge, or you too will be judged. For in the same way you judge others, you will be judged, and with the measure you use, it will be measured to you. "Why do you look at the speck of sawdust in your brother's eye and pay no attention to the plank in your own eye? How can you say to your brother, 'Let me take the speck out of your eye,' when all the time there is a plank in your own eye? You hypocrite, first take the plank out of your own eye, and then you will see clearly to remove the speck from your brother's eye."* If we judge in such a way that is condemning, then we ourselves will be judged in the same way! I love how bold Jesus was. He spoke such a simple truth but, it literally pierced down to the core. It's so true though! Jesus reveals to us that the sin in our brother's eye that we keep pointing out, is literally a speck of sawdust, which is not that big at all, but then tells us that our issues are the size of a log! Jesus is pretty much telling us that we have our own issues to work out. It's real hard to see anything when we have a 2x4 in our eye! Which is why we need to quit worrying about other people's issues and focus on what we need to do in order to better ourselves.

Self-righteousness

I remember as God began to open doors for me, I started to see things that I had been praying for come to pass. My wife and I arrived at Harvest Time Church and things were exploding, revival was happening, we had gotten our own place to live, great jobs, and this book was underway. God was doing big things, not just in the natural, but especially the spiritual. But I had this thought in the back of my mind. You ever have that thought, *"This is too good to be true?"* Yea, that's what I was thinking about. I think we have all experienced that, where things are going great and then BAM, something happens and it shakes your foundation. It's almost like we convince ourselves that we cannot live in victory forever. And I totally understand that we will not live this life free from trial and tribulation, but let me say this: bad days will come, but your good tomorrow is determined by how you react to your bad today.

As all these amazing things were happening, my good friend, Shane, spoke to me, *"Some people's temptations to fall is alcohol, drugs, or even pornography, but you will be attacked with pride. Pride will be your downfall if you are not aware."* As I sat there and dwelled on what he said, I had flashbacks of so many leaders I knew and heard of, who fell because of pride. I did not want that to be me.

Fast-forward two months and I am speaking at my church. My job was to transition from worship to tithe/offering and then into announcements. Personally for me, it is sometimes hard to transition from worshipping God to going right into greeting because, you just want to sit in the glory of God and the atmosphere worship has created. As I was speaking I had gotten distracted by something that was still going on in the front. I don't know exactly what happened but, I was drawing blanks in my mind. I began to stutter a little and I kept losing focus. It's like this thick cloud came over me.

I could feel myself getting nervous and my mouth start to dry out. Most of the time, I am very confident in my speaking because, I just let God do His thing. But it almost felt like the connection between God and I was cut. In all honesty, I felt stupid. I literally felt like I became dumb. I handed the mic over to my pastor and went to the back of the sanctuary. What just happened? I felt like a spirit of stupid came upon me. And if I am being honest, I was at a loss for words during most of the sermon. I was beating myself up because I felt like I embarrassed myself up there. I could hear the enemy saying, "*Pastor isn't going to want to use you anymore because you are a mess.*" I thought maybe he was right; I do feel like a mess. I tried to shrug it off multiple times but nothing really changed.

As the message was over and the speaker began the alter call, I walked to the side along with the prayer team, thinking to myself, "*I can't pray for these people. I am so messed up right now.*" And I remember thinking to myself that I need prayer, but the moment I said that, all these thoughts rushed into my head, "*I can't tell anyone about this. I am a leader; people are looking up to me. I will look weak and who wants prayer from a weak person?*" Just as I was thinking that the Lord reminded me of what Shane said, "*Pride will be your downfall if you are not aware.*"

I immediately turned to my buddy, Gilbert, and told him to pray for me. My wife, Gilbert, and two other leaders, laid hands on me and prayed for me before we began to minister to those who had stepped up to the front. Immediately, I felt God's presence. It was like someone plugged me back in and I felt that electricity flow through me. The stupidity I had felt was gone, but most importantly of all, I had just defeated an attack of pride.

Honestly, I don't know why I am writing this. I literally added this story at the last minute because I wanted you to know something: pride, many times, can be our greatest enemy when we are growing and God is using us. It's so easy, if we are not careful, to get pulled away by pride, which is directly connected to jealousy and envy. The Bible even tells us that God opposes the proud but gives grace to the humble (**James 4:6**). I was spoken over in Georgia before I left, and my friend told me, "*Your humility will be your platform.*" I have taken that to heart because, the only way God can use me fully is if I am full of Him and completely empty of pride.

When we are growing from level to level and God is speaking to us, the enemy will come and speak to you to try and get you jealous or envious of someone else's platform or influence. Pride can lead to many things, including a hardened heart, which makes it hard to hear God. Just like my situation, pride tried to step in and, because I was thinking about MY confusion and MY mess ups, I lost focus of why I even speak: to glorify God. Much like Peter when Jesus invited him to walk on water, the moment we take our focus off of HIM and onto the DISTRACTIONS (wind and waves) around us, we began to sink.

I very well could have kept that attack to myself and tried to play it off as if I have it all together, but what good would I have been if I was slowly dying of the disease called SELF. Falling does not define you, it's how you respond to your fall. Will you get up and shake it off? Or will you stay down? Will you let the falls dictate your future and identity? Will you seek help?

Self-inflicted

We always talk about how we as Christians can be so critical towards others, critical towards God, and even critical towards the devil, blaming him for way more than he has actually done (you're just giving him more attention than he deserves), but there is one person who receives the most criticism and the most judgement: ourselves. Yup, that's right, we sometimes are the most critical towards ourselves, causing a self-pity, false humility, and a negative perception of our identity. The devil has done a great job at coming in and deceiving us about, not only God's identity, but how we see ourselves, ultimately taking the focus off Jesus and the cross, and making us forget what Jesus' death really gave us. We have all done it. We have all grabbed a hold of this false identity that we are worthless, dirty, and unworthy. And yes, we sin, and yes, without God we are nothing, but there is one thing we must remember, WE HAVE GOD. We must remember the cross, because it did so much more than just forgive us of our sins, it redeemed us, gave us a new nature, which means we have a new identity in Christ Jesus.

So let me ask you, how do you view yourself? Do you identify as more of a sinner than you do a child of the King? Are you always focusing on the bad parts of your Christian walk than you are at what Jesus did for you? As I wrote in my previous book, we tend to take on the identity of "Sinner saved by grace," which is true, but when God looks at us He doesn't see a sinner saved by grace, He sees forgiven, He sees loved, He sees redeemed, and He sees Jesus in us, which is where we get our righteousness from. The enemy is going to come into your life and start questioning you in two areas: if you know who God is and if you know who you are. He did it with Eve and he continues to do it now.

My dog, Sophia used to have this old tennis ball and it was so dirty, so beat up, and so chewed up. It literally had a hole the size of a walnut on one side. It was discolored, used and bruised. It was her favorite toy, which would explain why it was in such bad shape. As I was staring at this ball one day, God began to speak to me about self-identity. You see, we were just like this tennis ball before Christ. We were messed up. We were used and abused. We were broken, lost, hurt, and rejected. We were sinners and that was our identity. Even after many of us got saved, religion taught us that Jesus death on the cross just "covered" our sins. Imagine putting some shiny tinfoil over that tennis ball and smoothing it all out. Yea, it looks real nice, but the sad truth is, deep down, under all that pretty wrapping, we are still just dirty sinners saved by grace, right? If we were to peel that away, we would uncover our nature that was there all along. And that is how many Christians see it, but that isn't the truth, in fact, the Bible says that Jesus didn't come and cover up our sins, it says that he BECAME our sin. **2 Corinthians 5:21** says, "*God made him who had no sin to be sin for us, so that in him we might become the righteousness of God.*" Jesus literally became sin. He became the curse for us (**Galatians 3:13**) He became the very thing that separated us from God. We were enemies to God, yet He still sent His son to die a death we deserved, becoming the very thing that damned us, and in exchange, Jesus gave us a new identity in and through Him.

Now, don't get me wrong, we still sin. I am not saying we will never sin, but even when we mess up and repent, God looks at us and He does not see sinner, in fact, when God looks at us He sees Jesus in us. He sees the righteousness of God in us. Why should we view ourselves any different? Religion has told us for so long that Jesus death on the cross was powerful, yet continuing to tell us that we are worthless and dirty, but which one is it? Are we worthless and unworthy? Or did Jesus' death on the cross truly make us a new creation? God has forgiven you, thrown your sin in the sea of forgetfulness—never to remember it again, why do you keep bringing it up then? We must learn to have mercy on ourselves as He has mercy on us. We must start seeing through the eyes of grace, not just others, but especially in the mirror.

And just to shift directions real quick, knowing who we are in Christ will also determine how we receive criticism from others as well. The way we respond to criticism pretty much depends on how we respond to praise. If the praise of men towards us humbles us, then criticism should build us up. But if praise inflates our heads and cause pride in us, then criticism will crush us, and both responses can so easily lead to our defeat. Just as critical words can tear us down if we are not rooted in Christ, we have to be careful of how we address issues as well. **Ephesians 4:29** tells us, "*Let no corrupting talk come out of your mouths, but only such as is good for building up, as fits the occasion, that it may give grace to those who hear.*"

The old has gone, behold, the new has come!

God spoke to me the other day and gave me two words as direction for this chapter, He said, "*RESTORE and REDIRECT.*" Through the truth of who God's word and what He has done for you, I pray that understanding redirects you to the right mindset and restores that which was once broken or distorted. You see, for too long we have been taught our identity from an orphan mindset instead of a son or daughter of the King. For too long we have had men and women on the pulpit, teaching their sheep who they are based off of their circumstances and lack, more than what Jesus did on the cross. For too long we have been told not to be so heavenly minded that we are no earthly good, but the truth is this: we HAVE to be heavenly minded in order to do good on this earth!

Has your phone ever froze on you and you had to do a hard reset? That's what I want to happen for those of us who have been taught traditions of our identity. Some of us need a hard reset. We have been stuck in life when it comes to love and identity, frozen due to an overload of false identity, and I want us to move back to the original place and mindset God created us to have. My desire for you is to get you to a place in your life where you can receive the fullness of Jesus' sacrifice on the cross. In all your getting, get understanding (**Proverbs 4:7**). In some versions it says, *"Though it cost all you have, get understanding."* Understanding this truth will truly set you free.

Matthew 16:24 tells us, *"If anyone would come after me, he must deny himself and take up his cross and follow me."* What does it mean to deny ourselves? It means we give up our own opinions of what we think is morally sound, we give up our rights and entitlements, and most importantly of all, we give up our past. You see, the truth will set us free, which means we have to break the lies because the lies bind us. We have people saying a quick little prayer and getting saved, which is amazing, yet we never tell people that we must now deny ourselves and pick up our crosses. Because of this, we have people saved but they are still haunted by their past, never really grabbing hold of the fact that we are literally brand new creations. I am going to end this with some scriptures that prove to you that you are brand new, that you are not just a sinner, and to show you that God looks at you and sees Jesus in you—He sees righteousness.

Romans 6:3-7 *Or don't you know that all of us who were baptized into Christ Jesus were baptized into his death? We were therefore buried with him through baptism into death in order that, just as Christ was raised from the dead through the glory of the Father, we too may live a new life. For if we have been united with him in a death like his, we will certainly also be united with him in a resurrection like his. For we know that our old self was crucified with him so that the body ruled by sin might be done away with, that we should no longer be slaves to sin- 7because anyone who has died has been set free from sin.*

Galatians 3:27- *for all of you who were baptized into Christ have clothed yourselves with Christ.*

Galatians 4:4-5- *But when the set time had fully come, God sent his Son, born of a woman, born under the law, to redeem those under the law, that we might receive adoption to sonship*

Hebrews 10:11-14- *Day after day every priest stands and performs his religious duties; again and again he offers the same sacrifices, which can never take away sins. But when this priest had offered for all time one sacrifice for sins, he sat down at the right hand of God, and since that time he waits for his enemies to be made his footstool. For by one sacrifice he has made perfect forever those who are being made holy.*

Galatians 2:16- *know that a person is not justified by the works of the law, but by faith in Jesus Christ. So we, too, have put our faith in Christ Jesus that we may be justified by faith in Christ and not by the works of the law, because by the works of the law no one will be justified.*

Colossians 1:19-22- *For God was pleased to have all his fullness dwell in him, and through him to reconcile to himself all* *things, whether things on earth or things in heaven, by making peace through his blood, shed on the cross. Once you were alienated from God and were enemies in your minds because of your evil behavior. But now he has reconciled you by Christ's physical body through death to present you holy in his sight, without blemish and free from accusation—*

1 Thessalonians 5:23-24- *May God himself, the God of peace, sanctify you through and through. May your whole spirit, soul and body be kept blameless at the coming of our Lord Jesus Christ. The one who calls you is faithful, and he will do it.*

Ephesians 1:7-9- *In him we have redemption through his blood, the forgiveness of sins, in accordance with the riches of God's grace 8 that he lavished on us. With all wisdom and understanding, he made known to us the mystery of his will according to his good pleasure, which he purposed in Christ,*

2 Corinthians 5:17- *Therefore, if anyone is in Christ, he is a new creation; the old things have passed away; behold, all things have become new.*

Colossians 3:5, Paul tells us, *"Put to death, therefore, whatever belongs to your earthly nature: sexual immorality, impurity, lust, evil desires and greed, which is idolatry. Because of these, the wrath of God is coming. You used to walk in these ways, in the life you once lived. But now you must rid yourselves of all such things as these: anger, rage, malice, slander, and filthy language from your lips. Do not lie to each other, since you have taken off your old self with its practices and have put on the new self, which is being renewed in the knowledge in the image of its Creator.*

THREE

WHO DO YOU SAY I AM?

Intro

The image and nature of God has been distorted by tradition since the crucifixion. We have always got our understanding of God more from our inexperience than our actual encounters with Him. When we see the sick we are told God only heals some. When we see the poor we are told God only blesses certain people, and when we see chaos we are told God controls every little aspect of our lives, so just buckle up and accept everything.

Throughout history, man's traditions have shaped God's character and nature, but I am here to show you God through our one and only true example: Jesus Christ. In this chapter we are going to look at scripture to prove God's nature—His good and loving, yet powerful nature. I will explain many things in this chapter, the biggest being the fact that Jesus is our best and most reliable source of knowing the Father, His will, and His character. Our entire Christian life is based off of a relationship with the Father, and sadly, many Christians only know about Him from tradition and religion. Our faith is not about religion, in fact, it's way more than a religion, it's relational.

The war on identity

One of the biggest areas that the enemy has attacked us in would have to be identity. Most would agree, I mean, look around. We live in a world where you can't hardly go a couple hours without seeing an image, video, status, or tweet that causes you to compare yourself and/or your ministry or church. It's true, our identity is under fire, but I want to take it a step further and a step deeper by saying this: the reason our identity is so shattered sometimes is because our idea of who God is and what His nature is like, has been completely distorted. We have Christians calling good evil and evil good, blaming God for things He never had a part of, and firing machine-gun prayers into the sky, just hoping one hits because you are not sure if he hears you or wants to move in your life.

May I be so bold as to say that before we can know who we are in Christ, we have to know who God is and what his nature and will is? **Ephesians 5:17** says, *"Therefore do not be foolish, but understand what the Lord's will is."* **Romans 12:2** tells us, *"Do not conform any longer to the patterns of this world, but be transformed by the renewing of your mind. THEN you will be able to test and approve what god's will is- his good, pleasing and perfect will."* In order for us to know God, we can no longer conform to the ways or patterns of this world. It's so easy to become so well-adjusted to our culture that we fit into it without even thinking. In order to know God's will, we must no longer conform to the world's patterns and we do so by renewing our minds! We do this by praying, reading, studying the word, worshiping God, and especially meeting with believers who challenge you, encourage you and build you up!

Here's the problem we are facing as a body; we have baby Christians (we all start somewhere), but they are not renewing their minds because they are being taught by casual and lukewarm Christians who are still conforming to the patterns of the world! This results in baby Christians staying immature Christians, and since they are not growing, they are still ignorant of God's will. But here is the worst part, those Christians then start ministries and churches and gather people together and start teaching casual, immature, lukewarm Christianity. And since there is no growth there is no life, and since there is no life there are no miracles, no healings, no deliverances, and surely no power! And so to explain why there is no growth or power in their church/life, they then explain it away and justify it by faulty theology about God's will for their lives and BOOM, the vicious cycle starts all over by church planting more casual, ignorant churches.

I'm not trying to sound rude, honestly, but it's the sad truth about what is really going on in American Christianity. And it's all because we do not know the true nature of the Father. We are afraid of and uncomfortable with signs, miracles, and casting out demons, so we throw them out instead of learning about them. And then we wonder why our congregation is saved but not set free. And because we only have partial truth to God's will and nature, we then only have partial truth of who we are in Christ.

The nature of God

There was a time when I used to wonder what God would be like if He was walking in the flesh with us right now. Who would He talk to? Who would He hangout with? What would his personality be like? Then it hit me, JESUS CHRIST! **Hebrews 1:3** says, *"The Son is the radiance of God's glory, and the EXACT representation of his being, sustaining all things by his powerful word."* Jesus only ever said what he heard the Father say and he only ever did what he saw the Father do (**John 5:19; John 12:49**). He said over and over again that him and the Father are the same and that the Son can do nothing by himself! Everything that Jesus said and everything that Jesus did was a display and a model of who the Father really is and what His will is for the world!

The Lord had spoken to me one morning and told me that we as Christians were never meant to be a people of confliction but, conviction. We are not only designed and commanded to know God and his nature/will, but we are given the opportunity to freely have an intimate relationship with him! We were never meant to be conflicted or confused about what he desires for our lives, yet that is one of the biggest battles we as Christians face today. According to **1 John 3:8**, Jesus came to destroy the devil's work! One of those works was confusion. The devil has been putting a veil over our eyes to blind us from God's character and nature, bringing confusion to our prayers, bringing confusion to our relationships, and bringing confusion to the way we respond to God! If we could just get over this hill of believing everything we hear from people, and just seek out God without any outer influence except the Word of God, you would find out real soon that God responds to us with His true nature and will. Jesus came to clear up any confusion of who the Father is, how much He loves you, and what His will is for every believer.

Who is Jesus to you?

On their way to the villages around Caesarea Philippi, Jesus asked this question out of the blue to his disciples, *"Who do people say I am?"* (**Matthew 16:13-20**) They replied, *"Some say John the Baptist; others say Elijah; and still others, Jeremiah or one of the prophets."* Jesus then turns the table and asks them the question of a lifetime, *"But what about you? Who do you say I am?"* Peter replied, *"You are the Christ, the Son of the Living God."* Friends, it doesn't matter who your parents say Jesus is, it doesn't matter who your auntie thinks Jesus is, in all honesty, it doesn't even matter who the world says Jesus is, Jesus is standing in front of you and asking the ultimate question, *"Who do YOU say I am?"* When you stand before God someday you will be by yourself and the only thing that's going to matter is who Jesus truly was to you!

Knowing who Jesus is will determine the manifestation of His power in your life. Don't believe me? Do you know what happened when Jesus returned to his hometown? He returned to his hometown and began to teach in the synagogue. At first people were amazed at his wisdom, but that amazement soon turned to offense as they began to ask questions; *"Where did he get these things? What's this wisdom that has been given him, that he even does miracles! Isn't this the carpenter? Isn't this Mary's son and the brother of James, Joseph, Judas and Simon? Aren't his sisters here with us?* **(Mark 6:2-3)"** Verse 5 says something that is powerful enough to shake your core, it says that, *"He could not do any miracles there, except lay his hands on a few sick people and heal them."* He was *literally amazed at their lack of FAITH* **(Vs. 6)**.

It's not that Jesus didn't have the power to heal all, it's that God is moved by our FAITH IN HIM. Their confliction about who Jesus really was, limited them and caused them to have no miracles manifest in their lives! They didn't see Jesus as the Messiah. They didn't see Him as the Healer, the Restorer, the Answer to life! All they could see was a carpenter, a former resident of Nazareth. And their lack of conviction resulted in a dry and dead faith. It literally says in verse 4 that they did not honor Jesus.

Are you starting to see a picture being painted of the importance of knowing who God is and what His will is for your life? I wholeheartedly believe that healing is for today, and it is true, it is, but it goes far beyond the physical. God wants to heal you and restore you in all aspects and in all realms of life.

Let me say something very bold here and I will prove it in scripture: If you do not have an understanding of who God's nature and will is, then you open the door for the enemy to kick you around! Go back to **Matthew 16** when Jesus asked his disciples who He was to them. After Peter responds to Jesus with the best answer possible, *"You are the Christ, the Son of the Living God"*, Jesus then replies, *"Blessed are you, Simon son of Jonah, for this was not revealed to you by man, but by my Father in heaven (***Vs. 17***) And I tell you that you are Peter, and on this rock I will build my church, and the gates of Hell will not overcome it. I will give you the keys of the kingdom of heaven; whatever you bind on earth will be bound in heaven, and whatever you loose on earth will be loosed in heaven."*

A whole religion has literally built their church on Peter, the saint, but completely missed what Jesus was actually saying here! Jesus isn't building His church on Peter, but the revelation Peter gets that JESUS IS THE CHRIST, THE SON OF THE LIVING GOD! When we have a true conviction and understanding, without a doubt, that Jesus is the healer, that Jesus is the Way, the Truth, and the Life, that Jesus is a restorer, redeemer, and a deliverer, THEN and only then will the gates of hell not prevail against the church! The enemy is beating the tar out of so many churches because their understanding of God's character and nature is like that of a boat in the stormy sea. *"The one who doubts is like a wave of the sea, blown and tossed by the wind* (**James 1:6**)" The next scripture literally tells us that a doubting man should not think he will receive anything from the Lord, that he is unstable in all he does! Wow, that is hard to swallow. I can honestly say that Christians are losing the battle because we doubt who God is and what He truly desires to do in our lives!

It saddens me so much to see Christians who struggle with identity, who are drowning in insecurities, and who go through their whole Christian walk getting hit on every side and thinking to themselves that this must be what Christianity is all about. Worst part is, many unbelievers are watching their lives and thinking, *"Why would I want that? I am better off in the world."* Yes, we will go through sufferings. Yes, we will go through trials and tribulation. But there is a difference between walking through the fire with Jesus and coming out not smelling like smoke, and walking through the fire and getting toasted!

I am willing

Luke 5:12-13 tells of a man with leprosy who fell before Jesus and said to him, *"Lord, IF you are willing, you CAN make me clean."* This man asked the question that so many of us are wondering sometimes. This man knew Jesus could heal. He knew he had the power to do anything! But the big confliction on his heart was whether Jesus was WILLING. So many of us know God is big and powerful. We know He is capable of healing us, we know He has the ability to restore us. God can take us out of debt, restore our marriage, comfort us in hard times, and give us a peace of mind... yet the question that lingers is whether He wants to or not. Listen to 80% of Christian's prayers when they pray for healing and you will hear, *"Lord, if it be your will."* They know He can, but they are not sure if that's what His will is or if He even wants to! Charles G. Finney was an amazing revivalist that was specifically keen on the prayer life of a Christian. He was quoted, saying, *"When God has specially promised something, we are bound to believe we shall receive it when we pray for it. You have no right to put in an 'if', and say, 'Lord, if it be thy will..." This is to insult God. To put an 'if' in God's promise when God has put none there, is tantamount to charging God with being insincere."* And even if we perceive that as a little harsh, we must come to a place in our lives when God's promises are absolute truth to us; His promises are YES and AMEN (**2 Corinthians 1:20**).

Before Finney gave his life to Christ, he would sit in on a church's prayer meetings, curious about what they were about. Something that always concerned Finney was a Christian's prayer life. He noticed that week after week, the prayers that they were offering were not being answered. He said, *"I understand from their utterances in prayer, and from other remarks in their meetings, that those who offered them did not regard them as answered."* Their lack of belief almost drove him to skepticism. He knew what the Bible promised, that if we ask, it shall be given; seek, and we shall find; knock, and the door will be opened (**Matthew 7:7-8**), but how they acted did not show that they believed! And as they asked him one night if they could pray for him, he shouted, *"No!"* and went on to say, *"because I do not see that God answers your prayers. I suppose that I need to be prayed for, for I am conscious that I am a sinner; but I do not see that it will do any good for you to pray for me; for you are continually asking, but you do not receive. You have been praying for revival ever since I came to Adams, and yet you have it not. You have* *been praying for the Holy Ghost to descend upon yourselves, and yet complaining of your leanness. You have prayed enough since I have attended these meetings to have prayed the devil out of Adams, if there is any virtue in your prayers. But here you are praying on, and complaining still.*"

If you have said this or still say this, then you're not alone, because I used to do the same thing. And that's probably why I never saw God move is because I knew He was God, but I was not convinced He was willing to move in my life. How did Jesus respond to this man who asked the question of a life time? He reached out his hand and touched the man saying, "*I am willing,*" he said, "*Be clean!*" *and immediately the leprosy left him.* (**Luke 5:13**)" Jesus is the same yesterday, today, and forever (**Hebrews 13:8**). Immediately following this verse in Hebrews, it tells us to not be carried away by all kinds of strange teachings: Jesus healed then and he is still healing and restoring today! He was willing then and he is willing now! Jesus is literally reaching his hand out to you right now and telling you that he is more than capable of healing you. He is more than capable to restore you. He is more than capable of taking away your anxiety. And not only is he telling you he CAN but, he is telling you he WANTS to. Maybe you're dealing with depression, maybe you have family issues, maybe you are having marital problems, or maybe you're facing literal death, Jesus wants to heal you, restore you, take care of you, and love on you. The death of Jesus was much more than just the forgiveness of sin; it was so we can experience heaven on earth.

But here's the deal, our healing is not just for ourselves. We are healed so we can go out and touch others. Just like we are blessed to be a blessing, God heals us because he loves us but also because he loves the people YOU can reach out to and pray for, love on, and lay hands on. I have seen so many people get healed and then turn around and continue in the life that Jesus died to save them from, and guess what, I literally watched their disease or sickness come back. I could literally write a whole other book on healing and how people can receive healing and how people can lose healing. It's true, but that's for another time.

Who am I?

"Define yourself as one radically beloved by God. This is the true self. Every other identity is an illusion." -Brennan Manning. The beautiful thing about knowing your true identity in Christ, and knowing your value, is that it always comes with purpose. This world is full of hurt people, who, without Christ, do not know who they truly are. We look for purpose and self-identity through drugs, sex, drinking, video games, sports, movies, and even relationships. If we never truly find our identity, worth, and purpose in Christ, then we will always find and worship a substitute God.

You see, many times when we think about giving our lives to Christ, a part of us has this idea that we will lose the best parts of ourselves; as if we will become a dull, not-as-fun version of who we are now. It's the identity that lukewarm

Christianity has given us—that Christianity is boring. But that's so far from the truth. C.S. Lewis talks about this in his book, "*The Screwtape Letters*," and says, "*When He [God] talks of their losing their selves, He means only abandoning the clamour of self-will; once they have done that, He really gives them back all their personality, and boasts (I am afraid, sincerely) that when they are wholly His they will be more themselves than ever.*" When we know who Christ is, we begin to know who we are, and when we start to give ourselves to Him, we become the man or woman that we were created to be, which is the best version of ourselves. The person we are in Christ is the most lovely, the most intelligent, the most giving, the most beautiful, and the funniest version of us.

For too long we have been trying to live life without a full revelation of who we are and how wonderfully made we are. The fear of man has fueled the fire of our insecurities. I am here to tell you that once we understand how God sees us through Jesus, we can stop caring what other people think about us. We can stop feeling bad about ourselves. We no longer have to seek the approval and praise of man because we already have the approval of our Father.

Becoming confident in who you are in Christ is a process. Every day we must come to know Him in order to be confident in self. Our goal is to be consumed by Christ. Once we do that, we find joy and purpose. I am not sure who said this, but I saw this quote one day and I feel it's appropriate to share in this section, "*To be in Christ, that is redemption; but for Christ to be in you, that is sanctification! To be in Christ, that makes you fit for heaven; but for Christ to be in you, that makes you fit for earth! To be in Christ, that changes your destination; but for Christ to be in you, that changes your destiny! The one makes heaven your home, the other makes this world His workshop."*

I want you to know something: when our foundation is set on Christ, no matter what happens, our identity will always be in Him. Contrary to popular belief, our identity is not in our happiness, and it's not in our suffering. Our identity is in Christ and Him alone, whether we are in joy or happen to be suffering. I say all of this because we as Christians need to step up and out of our false identities and truly start walking in the identity that Jesus died to give us. You are forgiven, redeemed, set free, chosen, set apart, called, blessed, righteous, washed clean, and loved! And until we learn to walk in these things, we can never truly influence the world. I honestly believe that the church is not influencing the world as it should because the church is being more influenced by the world. We need to come to a place where, in Him we live and move and have our entire being (**Acts 17:8**).

As we begin to truly uncover God's nature through Jesus Christ's life, we start to get a better understanding of our identity through His sacrifice. **John 1:11-13** says, "*He came to His own, and His own did not receive Him. But as many as received Him, to them He gave the right to become children of God, to those who believe in his name: who were born, not of blood, nor of the will of the flesh, nor the* *will of man, but of God.*" As we study scripture, the Holy Spirit is painting a picture of true Christianity; the more we study, read, and God reveals to us, the more of the painting we see. The more we study Jesus' life, death, and resurrection, the more we start to comprehend our identity through everything that He died to give us. When we receive Jesus as Savior, a beautiful thing happens: We are transformed and made new. When we believe in Him, He gives us a right to become His children. We become born of God. Our spiritual DNA changes from the world, to Christ. The more we encounter Him, the more our thoughts, words, and lifestyle changes.

All throughout Jesus' ministry, we see a picture coming together; hints of what Jesus has done for us through the words He spoke and the miracles He did, starting with His very first miracle in **John 2**: turning water into wine. At first glance, it doesn't seem like a huge miracle compared to healing the sick, but there is a visual that I saw through this miracle that I want to share. "*Now there were set there six waterpots of stone, according to the manner of purification of the Jews, containing twenty or thirty gallons apiece. Jesus said to them, "Fill the waterpots with water." And they filled them up to the brim. And He said to them, "Draw some out now, and take it to the master of the feast." And they took it. When the master of the feast had tasted the water that was made wine, and did not know where it came from (but the servants who had drawn the water knew), the master of the feast called the bridegroom. And he said to him, "Every man at the beginning sets out the good wine, and when the guests have well drunk, then the inferior. You have kept the good wine until now*!"

There are three things I want you to see, 1) there were six stone jars, six is the number of man, 2) Jesus wants his disciples to fill them with water and they did so, filling them to the brim, and 3) Jesus transformed the water into GOOD wine. We represent those waterpots, and when Jesus comes into our lives, he fills us up with, not just any regular water but, Himself, the Living Water, and not just half way, but to the brim! This new life that Jesus promises us, through his death and resurrection, is not just a casual thing. He is taking broken, dirty, old vessels, and filling us to the brim with His LIFE, and then transforming us into something new and into something good! Jesus just didn't make ok wine, or kind-of-good wine, He made the BEST wine.

I feel as if He was not only being obedient to his mother, but also giving the world a small taste of what He came to do and who he came to do it for. The more we begin to see Jesus for who He really is, the more we will see who we were created to be, leading us into a more confident, mature Christianity.

Not everything that happens, is God's will

The New Testament makes it crystal clear that not everything that happens is God's will. For example, Jesus instructed his disciples to pray that God's will would be done on earth (**Matt. 6:10**). If everything that happens is God's will, such prayer is superfluous. In **Romans 1:10**, Paul said he prayed for "*a prosperous journey in the will of God*" to see the believers there. Another meaningless prayer? No. The will of God for an individual, whether revealed in the written Word of God or by direct revelation, generally comes to pass only when that person understands it and, by his own, acts accordingly. It's crazy how we have been convinced that everything that happens is orchestrated by God. From storms to death, to even stubbing your toe! Let me give you a little revelation: God is all-powerful, all-seeing, he is everywhere all at once, BUT people seem to forget one of the biggest things he set in motion when He created us: FREE WILL. He has given us free choice, which is honestly why our world is in the state it is in. We as humans tend to make selfish, greedy, ignorant choices at times, even Christians do it. And although God is everywhere, he doesn't force himself into relationship with us, we have our end to keep up on that.

I am not taking away from God's power; I'm just speaking common truth here. It takes true strength and relationship to stand up during a tragedy and not blame God, because honestly, that is usually our go-to answer when tragedy hits, we blame God. It's the easy thing to do when we don't understand a situation. We as humans HAVE to know everything, and when we don't understand something we pull an answer out of a hat that makes us feel better about our situation. Trust me, I totally understand. I have been through some stuff, I have been confused on why it happened, and I have been tempted to run to God and ask Him why he let this happen, but I had a foundation rooted in me that taught me to know God, examine myself, and the one big truth: sometimes we just don't know things.

In 2017 my wife and I hit a very rough time in our lives. We had a miscarriage. I won't go into too much detail, but long story short, we were excited when we found out my wife, Leana, was pregnant. But about 4-6 weeks in something terrible happened. Sitting in the emergency room at 4am, my wife in the hospital bed next to me, I was faced with one question: why? Why would this happen? Did we do something wrong? Why did her body reject our baby? What could we have done to change things?

The questions flooded my mind and I felt like the most helpless husband in the world. It was hard for a while. My wife and I will never be the same. The worst part though? Talking to Christians. Yes, talking to Christians was always so cringe-worthy because, like I said, we as humans always feel the need to say the right thing and fix things, especially when the best thing to do is just be quiet. We heard the normal Christianese response, *"God has a plan for this,"* or, *"God is in control,"* and all I wanted was for them just to be present. Even though these comments had truths to them, they were vague and did not pertain to this situation. Why? Because God did not take our baby. God did not do this because "He wanted to teach us something." God is not controlling every decision we as humans make. Sometimes things happen, sometimes it's our fault, sometimes things just don't play out like we hoped it would. We live in a fallen world full of sin. The best piece of advice I ever got was that sometimes we will not know why something happened, and that's ok. It's ok not to know. It's ok to tell people that you really have no idea why this happened. We always want an answer, whether it's truly biblical or not.

One thing that truly sustained Leana and I after everything that happened was understanding that God wasn't our problem, but our answer. When crisis happens we always question God and we have a tendency to blame Him. During these times our concept of His nature begins to blur. I had someone ask me, "*Why did that happen to you guys? You guys are good people.*" My response was this: "*We are human. Sometimes we miss it. Sometimes we don't listen. Sometimes we let fear get the best of us. Sometimes bad things happen. I can't tell you exactly why all this happened, but one thing I do know is this: God is good and He is my answer. He is my healer and the One who restores us.*"

God is not our problem, friends. He is our answer, our loving Father who adores us, the One who brings life and life more abundantly. The enemy wants to create division between you and the Father to disconnect you from your one and only true answer. Do not build walls between yourself and God. Do not distance yourself. Do not question yourself into depression. Turn to the Father and let Him comfort you. "*A thief has only one thing in mind—he wants to steal, slaughter, and destroy. But I have come to give you everything in abundance, more than you expect — life in its fullness until you overflow!*" -**John 10:10** TPT

I tell you this because the wrong idea of God's nature will eventually drive you away. I have watched so many Christians believe God was responsible for the death of their child, and in doing so, they got mad at God, putting up a wall between them and their only true answer to hope. They then slowly fall away from Him, holding grudges that should have never been towards him. Before you know it, you no longer care about God, church, or anything that has to do with Christianity. It's funny how we blame the devil for all these little things in life, but when big tragedy comes, we always look to God. I am not going to pretend I know everything, but I just look at Jesus and his nature and I see nothing but life, love, and restoration. I don't see death and destruction. And if Jesus is the Father's nature, then that's who He has always been, even in those scriptures where it doesn't make sense. I believe we all have a lot to learn and grow in, as for me, I will stand before God one day and tell him how I told the masses that He was a good and loving God. What will you say?

I want you to understand that there are three forces at play in this world. Some things happen because God orchestrates it, some things happen through the devil's influence, and other things happen because we are enticed by our own evil desires, which give birth to sin (read **James 1**), but no matter what happens, if we are willing to seek God, He can teach us and grow us through any of those situations.

Romans 8:28 says, *"And we know that all things work together for good to those who love God, to those who are the called according to His purpose."* Just because God can cause all things to work together, doesn't mean He caused all things. There is a quote from, *"The Shack,"* that says, *"Just because I work incredible good out of unspeakable tragedies doesn't mean I orchestrate the tragedies. Don't ever assume that my using something means I caused it or* *that I need it to accomplish my purposes. That will only lead you to false notions about me. Grace doesn't depend on suffering to exist, but where there is suffering you will find grace in many facets and colors."* The amazing thing about God is, that no matter what happens in our lives, He has an answer. If we let Him, He can take any situation, any trauma, any loss, and He can bring life out of it. Whether He has placed something in your life, the devil is tempting you, or you get yourself in a mess, God can teach you and mold you through it all, and you can come out stronger and more mature than ever.

My wife has become a beacon of hope to any woman that has experienced what she did. She now can encourage and build up other women around her. She can be exactly what she didn't have, and what she needed, to those who are going through the same situation; who may be asking the same questions I did. And maybe now, she can help prevent certain things that she didn't have to go through. *"Praise be to the God and Father of our Lord Jesus Christ, the Father of compassion and the God of all comfort, who comforts us in all our troubles, so that we can comfort those in any trouble with the comfort we ourselves have received from God."* – **2 Corinthians 1:3-4**

Grace doesn't need suffering to be known, but whenever you find yourself in a storm, you better believe His grace is there, available, and sufficient!

FOUR

FAITH AND HEALING

Intro

If there is one area that has truly been distorted and thrown out, it's the fact that God is not only ABLE to heal, but it's the fact that He is WILLING to heal. As far as I can remember, from the first time coming to church in 7th grade, to 17 years later, healing had always been an up and down topic. I would see people praying for healing, then act as if they were going to die. I didn't know much about faith and healing then, but one thing I remember thinking is how chaotic Christians were with their beliefs. Sometimes they would say God is a healer and full of love, then they would be blaming Him for cancer and a little boy dying. It confused me so much. I didn't know what to believe.

It wasn't until I began to study out the Bible for myself that I started to see a pattern throughout scripture: God's whole mission and purpose is to restore what the enemy destroys. From Genesis all the way to Revelations, God wants to bring life, while the enemy wants to steal, kill and destroy (**John 10:10**). I began to understand that the traditions of men had literally conformed God's nature to their circumstances. We were no longer getting our source of

God's nature and will from the Holy Scriptures, but from our experiences and even inexperience.

I dare you to read this chapter with a child-like faith. Clear your mind of any confusion that tradition may have taught you. Look to the Word and look to Jesus, who is the Word made flesh, and He will show you exactly what the Father's will is for healing in your life. It's time we die to the traditions of men and come to life in God's divine healing.

Knowing His nature

When we began to know God's nature and his will, our prayers stop sounding like a question and more like a statement. We stop saying things like, *"If it be your will,"* because now we are confident that it is. Let me ask you something, if we know the Bible says he hears our prayers (**1 John 5:15**), and if the Bible tells us that Jesus, who is the nature of God, healed ALL (**Acts 10:38**), and if the Bible states that whatever we ask in Jesus' name, he will do it for us (**John 14:13-14**), then why do we keep praying the same prayer over and over again as if God didn't hear us or, as if the more we pray the better chance it comes to pass? In reality, if we truly believed what we prayed the first time, then all our prayers following that should be us praising God and thanking him. When we talk about prevailing in prayer, we are talking about prayer that secures an answer. Just saying prayers is not necessarily offering prevailing prayer, in fact, the prevalence of prayer does not depend so much on quantity as on quality.

Let me ask you, what is faith? Faith is the substance of things hoped for, the evidence of things not seen (**Hebrews 11:1**). So, faith is having a hope and a confidence of the EVIDENCE of the things NOT YET seen. CJ, that's makes no sense. Let me put it this way, if you asked your earthy dad for a new car and he said yes, then what do you do after that? Do you continue to ask him for a car? No, you don't. You start thanking him every time you see him because you have a confidence that, since your dad told you yes, you will see that car. You are confident that the car is coming, even though you have not seen it yet. Same way with God. There's nothing wrong with things on God's end, it's us. How many times do we pray for healing or a breakthrough and we turn around and we start telling people how sick we are instead of how God is a healer? Or we ask God for something and then start making our own plans to obtain it because, deep down, we truly do not believe God will do it. Let's be real with ourselves here, friends. There are so many things that God has already given us, yet we continue to pray and ask for it constantly (see **2 Peter 1:3**). The prison door is open, yet we just sit in our cell asking God to free us. Once you start seeing things in this light, your whole prayer life changes, which leads to a change in your everyday life.

Faith is a HUGE part of our daily walk. A lot of times we blame God in a very Christinese way for things he isn't responsible for at all. We say things like, "*God is in control*," a very vague statement, that inconspicuously shifts the responsibility off us and puts it on God. And just so you know, He is in control, but he isn't a puppeteer, pulling all the strings. God is all-powerful and he holds the universe together, but that phrase has become a vague, poor answer to the unknown in our lives. This makes it so we don't have to use faith. It's a cop-out, because a lot of the times we think it's too hard to have faith and believe for the things of God. But the fact of the matter is, faith is a key component to seeing the manifestations of God in our lives. In fact, there were multiple healings during Jesus' ministry that were a direct result of a person's faith (**Mark 10:52; Mark 5:34; Luke 17:19**). And even more than that, a lack of faith actually limited the amount of healings Jesus performed in his own hometown (**Mark 6:6**). Jesus even said to Jairus, "*Do not be afraid; just have FAITH*," (**Mark 5:36**)

The longer I walk with God, the more I start to see how little we as Christians look at faith. We think of faith as just "hoping" for something, but it's so much more than that. Faith is a force at work that can literally move God to manifest in your life. Faith is huge. In fact, faith, combined with our words, is how we got saved in the first place. We believe in heart and confess with our mouth (**Romans 10:9**). But it goes beyond just salvation. Faith activates the kingdom, especially when it comes to healing. In fact, faith is so important, **Luke 18:8** asks the question of a lifetime: "*when the Son of Man comes, will he find faith on the earth?*" Let me ask you something, God is looking for a people who have faith in him, do you have faith? Will God find faith in your life? And I am talking about mountain moving, city shaking faith. I am talking about the faith that believes God can do HUGE things, even impossible things!

I know people who have literally had people give them cars. And it's not just, "*Here, here is another car even though you already have three*," No, these people had no car, no way to work, no way to the store, their circumstances looked bad, yet they knew without a doubt that God would provide and BAM, someone gives them a car because God told them to. THAT'S the kind of faith God wants to see on the earth from his children.

Healing is a topic I could write a whole book about. There so much to it. So many of us see healing as black or white, but there are many things that can influence our healing, and there are many things that can hinder our healing. I have seen people lose their healing just as fast as they got it. One of those deciding factors that can invite healing into your life is FAITH. Jesus made some pretty bold statements about what will happen for the one who believes. "*Very truly I tell you, whoever believes in me will do the works I have been doing, and they will do even greater things than these, because I am going to the Father* (**John 14:12**)." This is Jesus that is talking here. Jesus' ministry has been nothing but love, healing, and deliverance up to this point, and now he is telling us that if you BELIEVE in him, you WILL do the works he has been doing, but here is the part that is the craziest, he says, "*even greater!*" What? I can hear a majority of believers yelling, "*Blasphemy!*," after reading that, but it's the truth. Jesus is saying that those who believe in him, those who have faith in him, those who are completely trusting in him, they will do the same exact ministry as what Jesus was doing, and even greater. How? Because the Holy Spirit, the very power of God, is in us!

That means God wants to live through you, love through you, heal through you, and cast out demons through you!

But here we are, American Christianity, where so many Christians will go out and watch scary movies and participate in Halloween, but when it comes to casting out demons and healing, they get freaked out and call those who BELIEVE weirdos. That's cool with me, you stay bound in your dead religion. I will just be over here living an abundant life and watching God set people free and heal them! Here's the bold truth that can be hard to swallow: if you don't believe in healing and deliverance, then there is a good chance you won't see it manifest in your life. Yes, God is merciful. Yes, His grace abounds, but there is also plenty of evidence that lack of faith and unbelief will limit the move of God in your life.

For me, I went to a church for 7 years of my life without ever hearing about any of this, and guess what, I never saw God move. I believe he was reaching out to me time after time, but I never knew that He was still in the signs and wonders business. The sad part was, no one ever came up to me and told me the truth until my second year of college. Long story short, I heard the true gospel for the first time and was childish enough to believe everything Jesus said. Life after that point has been absolutely amazing. The biggest revelation I ever got was knowing that Jesus didn't just die for my sins, in fact, he died for so much more. He died to redeem us from the curse and he died to bring us restoration in all areas. Christians tend to forget about the full aspect of communion: we drink the wine (or juice) to remember the forgiveness of sins, but what about the bread? His body was broken, but why? If the blood is for sins, then what would the point of his body breaking for us? It was for our healing!

I had a friend one time ask me to pray for them because they were sick. As I was getting ready to pray and ask God to heal them, He spoke to me so clearly, saying, "*So many times my people are asking for a miracle healing, but sometimes their healing is not in a miracle at all, but in wisdom.*" In other words, we are always on the go, always doing something, our diets are off and we are so stressed out about money and life, and so we ask God for a miracle healing but God is telling us that we don't need a miracle, we just need to rest, slow down, eat better, and maybe step away from the checkbook! As I studied to be a paramedic years ago, I came to the realization that everyday stress can cause your body so much physical damage. Isn't that crazy? Thoughts in the mind can literally cause physical damage to our bodies! And what makes things worse is that we continue to live these crazy lives to the point where we are physically hurting and then we run to God and ask Him to heal us, and when he does, then we turn around and do it all over again, almost expecting different results.

I can honestly say that I was one of those people that never stopped doing things, but I kept confessing that I can do all things through Christ! Yet my body felt like I got hit by a bus. God spoke to me one day and said, '*I cannot bless what is not of me.*" And I was like, "*What do you mean? I am doing all these things for you!*" And he replied, "*I never told you to do all these things. Yes, I am merciful. Yes, I am graceful, but I also gave you wisdom and discernment to decide what is permissible and what is beneficial.*" He reminded me of **1 Corinthians 10:23** that says, "*All things are lawful,*" but not all things are helpful. "*All things are lawful,*" but not all things build up." Yes, we can do all these things, great, but are they helpful? Do they build up? Are they even from God? We as a society glorify business, and that lifestyle may cause some issues, and I believe that God is wanting us to use wisdom, be smart, and rest! I feel like so many of our sicknesses are caused by US. I honestly feel like we could be healed if we just changed our mindset and changed our lifestyle. So maybe you have been praying for a miracle healing and you haven't seen any results yet. I believe God is speaking to some of you and He is telling you to just rest, not only in the physical, but in the spiritual; rest in God, because when we live through God and learn to rest in Him, life never really seems like work.

Out of context

There is this story of a woman whose daughter was very sick. A pastor had gotten in contact with her and began to minister to her. He explained how God was a healer and how he was not only able but, willing to heal her daughter. She had replied back and thanked him for his words but she had already come to the conclusion that God had planned this life for her and her daughter and that they have accepted it. She then ended the message **with 1 Corinthians 2:9**, which says, "*No eye has seen, no ear has heard, and no mind has imagined what God has prepared for those who love him.*"

Some of you guys reading this have probably used this scripture so many times in your life, but it's out of context. I want you to read the very next verse. Verse 10 says, "*But God has revealed it to us by the Spirit. The Spirit searches all things, even the deep things of God.*" The reason why this saddened me so much is because this woman based her entire theology about her daughter's healing on an out-of-context scripture. THIS is why I wrote this book. Men have passed down tradition after tradition and Christian's have grabbed hold of it and ran with it. You see it all the time! Cliché Instagram pictures, Facebook posts, and vague tweets have become Christian's "daily devotions," and have created whole theologies! They pray for healing and breakthrough and don't see it within hours and so they turn to social media to feed their fears and doubts, trying to find a post that gives their situation meaning.

I am not bashing this woman because I literally lived like this for the first seven years of my Christianity! I believed whatever came my way because I never bothered developing a relationship with God and I never tried reading my Bible. I have no idea what happened to this woman or her daughter, but it sparked a fire in me to set out and speak the truth even more.

I came across this video on Facebook of a Christian filmmaker by the name of Jacob Dufour. He went on this Christian Facebook page to promote his films and noticed that so many people were just saying amen to anything and everything that sounded good. There were even a lot of "*Like for Jesus, keep scrolling for Satan.*" Just ignorant things like that. It sparked an idea in his head to really put

Christians to the test. He created an image that said, "*If you worship me all will be yours.*" **Luke 4:7**. *Amen if you agree.*" If you read this verse, it's not Jesus talking, but the devil tempting Jesus! But he wanted to see if Christians really read their word.

After 1 minute he had 5 "amens" After an hour he had over 100 comments and "amens." Later that day he had over 600 likes and 576 comments, and out of all these comments and likes, only 20 people corrected him. If you calculate that, that's 3.5% that knew where this verse came from. That means almost 97% of Christians who read this agreed with something straight from the devil's mouth because it sounded good and was taken out of context. And the one thing that really got me was one of the posts came from a pastor. This young man commented and asked him if he was a pastor and he said, "*yes.*" He replied, "*Do you know who is saying this?*" The pastor replied, "*Yes... our Lord Jesus.*" That right there really got me, because THIS is what's wrong with Christianity. This is the reason I felt God wanted me to write this book. We have all done it before too. We grab onto something because it sounds good and makes us feel good, but we never read our Bible to find out if what we believe is even biblical. I feel like a repeating record here but this is important, friends. We have to study our Bible. We have to develop a relationship with the Lord. The reason I titled this book, "*More Than a Religion,*" is because in order to truly become an effective Christian in this life we must have a relationship with the Lord. It's not enough to say that we know of God, there has to be healthy fruit in your life that proves that you have what you say you have. Let me break this down for you.

Every relationship we have either has healthy fruit or unhealthy fruit. It either has healthy growth or unhealthy growth. Unhealthy relationships produce unhealthy fruit in your life. No matter what relationship you enter in, whether good or bad, you never are the same person you were when you first started. Let's use my wife and I as an example. I am not the same man I was when I first met Leana. I am not even the same man I was when we got married over 3 years ago. Our healthy relationship has grown deeper, our intimacy is greater, our understanding of who we are is greater, and our love for each other is deeper. It has to be the same way with God. If we truly have a relationship with God, then we shouldn't be the same person we were when we first entered that relationship. Our intimacy with God should be greater, our understanding of His nature should be expanded, and our love for Him should have grown deeper and deeper. Relationship with the Father is the center of our Christian faith. And as I said, if we claim we have something, then there must be healthy fruit to prove it. When we don't read our Bibles and we don't have a strong foundation of who God is or who we are or why we believe what we believe, then we will fall into any false teaching that comes our way.

1 Peter 3:15 gives us a beautiful reminder, *"But in your hearts revere Christ as lord. Always be prepared to give an answer to everyone who asks you to give the reason for the hope that you have. But do this with gentleness and respect."* How many Christians have you talked to that really don't know if they are going to heaven? How many of us can actually answer why we believe what we believe or why Jesus died for us? We are called to give an answer to why we believe what we believe. Do you know why Jesus died for you? Do you know what He died to GIVE you? Do you know if you are going to heaven? Do you honestly know why you believe what you believe? I encourage you, if you don't know the Bible or find yourself lacking answers; read, study, and pray. Study the Bible, listen to anointed preachers, and ask questions. If you don't have a strong foundation, you will fall for anything. I will end this section with this scripture about the importance of growing with God, but also how your relationship with God is also determined by who you surround yourself with.

Ephesians 4:11, "*So Christ himself gave the apostles, the prophets, the evangelists, the pastors and teachers, to equip his people for works of service, so that the body of Christ (you) may be built up until we all reach unity in the faith and in the knowledge of the Son of God and become mature, attaining to the whole measure of the fullness of Christ. Then we will no longer be infants, tossed back and forth by the waves, and <u>blown here and there by every wind of teaching and by the cunning and craftiness of people in their deceitful scheming</u>.*" In some versions it says, "*tossed and blown about by every wind of NEW TEACHING (or doctrine).*" Going to the right church and being surrounded by the right, anointed people, will build us up and prepare us, so that we can reach unity in the faith and deepen our understanding of who Jesus us, maturing in all areas, so that we will no longer be babies, but instead we will have a foundation that will establish us and strengthen us so that we are not tossed around by every false doctrine that comes our way. When false teachings or out of context scriptures come our way, we can stand firm and know God's truth!

We need to learn what to receive and what to rebuke, and when we grow closer to God, we will know without a doubt!

The "what ifs" of healing

As I write this section, I am currently in San Antonia, TX for a friend's wedding. Anytime I travel I always pray for ministering opportunities. I may take vacations but I never vacation from the great commission. And just like any vacation you take, it wouldn't be a complete getaway unless you stop by a Starbucks. What I love about Starbucks is how busy they are, which usually means a lot of people who could use prayer. As I was walking in this Starbucks in downtown San Antonio, I noticed a man sitting outside on crutches. As I waited in line to order my drink, I noticed he was getting up and limping over to the door and holding it for people. I could tell he had been on the streets, but the thing I noticed most about him was that he never once was asking anyone for anything, just telling people, *"God bless you."* I began to have a battle in my mind as I felt God tug on my heart to pray over his ankle. My spirit was like, *"Yes! Go love on him and pray over him!"* But my flesh was asking questions, *"What if he doesn't receive? What if you pray over him and nothing happens? What if you make you and God look like a bunch of fools!?"*

As I started to dwell on the thought of him not getting healed, I asked a question many of us ask, *"What if he doesn't get healed?"* My question to you, *"What if he does?*" We cannot let the fear of "what if" paralyze us from ever stepping out and praying for people. None of us want to stand back on our life and wonder what it would have been like if we had stepped out and said that encouraging word or prayed over that person.

I ordered my drink and walked outside and began asking him what happened to his ankle. He told me his story and we talked a little bit about a couple things. I asked him if he was saved and he said yes, he believed in Jesus and had been baptized and everything. Long story short, I laid hands on his ankle and prayed healing over him. I prayed that he would find work soon and that the Lord would touch him. After I prayed, I chatted with him and told him a little bit about what faith was and how I wanted him to continue to confess his healing and praise God. I walked away excited but at the same time I was a little discouraged. Did he feel anything? Did he get healed? Did any of that minister to him? And that's when God spoke to me and told me that he was speaking to that man and bringing comfort to him as we speak. You see, sometimes we think that everything is going to be these huge miracles, like a burning bush appearing before you and saying, *"Congrats, the healing has worked. Well done,"* but it's not always going to be like that. I may not have seen this man jump up and start running around, although things like this happen often around the world, and the Bible confirms God's will to heal, but that doesn't mean God is not working in this man's life. And besides, whether he did or not, my job is to be obedient, not heal him.

I walked away not seeing certain things in the natural, but

in the spiritual there were seeds being sown and maybe a confirmation taking place. I don't know everything and I can't answer every concern out there, but what I do know is that, just because we may not see things in the natural, doesn't mean that healing isn't happening or that person isn't being set free in one way or another.

The enemy has done a great job at convincing us it's better for us to never try than to try and fail, but that could be farther from the truth. As you read the Bible, you see a confidence from Paul and Peter and the other believers, not only because they heard about God's goodness, but because they have had true encounters with God. There was a reason I used to be so stiff when it came to worship, and there was a reason I was so afraid to step out and pray for people, and that reason was because I lacked a true, intimate relationship with the Lord; where I encountered him constantly. The more we get to know God, the more confident we are of His nature and love for those around us. Fear of failing still tries to stop you, but now you have a foundation and a wisdom that knows what God desires. It helps knowing that we are not the healer, God is! We are just the vessel that God flows through. God is looking for our obedience!

In **Acts 4**, Peter and John just got done laying hands on crippled beggar and he was instantly healed. The religious leaders did not like this and had them thrown in jail. The next day they began to question them and asking them by what name were they doing this? "*It is by the name of Jesus Christ of Nazareth that this man stands before you healed* (**Acts 4:10**)." I love their boldness here. They knew where the true source of their power came from. Yes, they were obedient, but God was the one that was doing the healings. They were confident because it was God's power doing all the work! Verse 13 says, *"When they saw the courage of Peter and John and realized they were unschooled, ordinary men, they were astonished and they took note that these men had been with Jesus. But since they could see the man who had been healed standing there with them, there was nothing they could say."* Peter and John were just ordinary men with faith in an amazing God. They were astonished at their courage and confidence, and that's what it's about, friends. They were confident and courageous because they had encounters with Jesus, leaving them forever changed. It literally said they, *"cannot help speaking about that they have seen and heard,"* (**Acts 4:20**). The more you begin to step out and pray for people, fearless about the outcome, confident in the God you serve and His power that flows through you, the more courageous you will become.

The disease of offense and self-pity

We tend to blame God when we don't see healing and restoration in our lives, but what if I told you that many times when we don't see healing in our lives it could be our own fault? I am convinced that the spirit of offense and self-pity has infiltrated the church and has caused so many of us to lose out on our healing because we are so self-absorbed. The enemy has literally stolen healing from so many believers because he has shifted the focus off of God, the Physician, and on to us. The tactic of the enemy is getting us offended, and then creating division and isolation from those who can help us, and then drowning us with self-pity, until we literally fall into depression. I have seen it over and over again. Let me be honest with you, I would rather have people in my life who are not afraid to tell me the truth, whether I get offended or not. I would rather have the people in my life who challenge me to get out of my circumstances, rather than those people who pat my back and make me comfortable in my pity party.

The enemy, many times, will try and get you offended to create division between you and those who can truly help you get out of your circumstances. Those people you have deemed, *"Too much,"* or, *"Too judgmental,"* are probably not judgmental at all, you are just easily offended. Those people may be the people who have the answer to your problems. The issue lies in the focus of our lives. We cannot be like the Israelites, who murmured and complained and because of it, death and destruction followed. Their 10 day trip turned into 40 years because they had to keep going around the mountain. (see **1 Corinthians 10**)

Beyond

Most of what I am writing to you God is teaching me right now. I have not arrived and I still make mistakes and struggle with believing God for big things. I am not going to sit here and pretend I am something I am not. Although, I am so much better than I used to be, I still have a lot of growing to do. We all do. But one thing God has been trying to do in my life is expand my faith and belief in him. My pastor in Georgia was talking to us in a staff meeting one day and telling us how God had placed the word, "Beyond," on his heart.

He began to explain how God wants to take us beyond where we are at. It was a word I never really used much in my vocabulary. A year and a half later and the Lord is bringing that word back to my attention. We as humans tend to think, believe, and live in such a small box. We set these tiny limits and these small boundaries and never allow God to truly work in our lives. I feel like God is shifting things in my life, and maybe he is doing the same for you, but I believe he is wanting to take us to the next level, beyond our human limit. He wants to take us out of our comfort zone, to a place that requires us to completely trust in him. God is wanting you to be in a place where His word is more real than any diagnosis or word from man.

We need to stop elevating man's words over God's. I praise God for good doctors, but God wants you to go beyond that diagnosis and believe that he is Jehovah Rapha, the Lord who heals all your diseases! He wants you to believe He is Jehovah Jireh, your Provider! God wants you to intimately know him as Jehovah Nissi, your Banner! It's time we change our mindsets, break down the walls of our fears and failures, and go above and beyond our boxes and mindsets that we let the world and lukewarm, casual religion plant in us! There is a place in faith where we have to step out and believe, especially when it doesn't make sense at all. And guess what, it may mean we need to unlearn some things that we picked up along the way. It means we are going to have to put our pride down, humble ourselves, and be willing to receive correction. Some of us are not going anywhere because we are just going to settle and believe the doctor's report, or believe our family when they tell us we will never amount to anything, or even believe the enemy when he tells us we are so unworthy.

Hebrews 11 tells us that, *"Faith is the substance (other versions say confidence) of things hoped for, the evidence of things not seen."* You remember the analogy of the car I used earlier? If we believe it, then our words and actions must line-up with our faith. If we do not know what God desires for us to have, then how are we going to believe for it? THIS is why it's so important, as I talked early in the book, to know God's nature, because in God's nature you find His character and His will. And if you are not confident in what God wills, then your prayers will be more like wishes than they will be confident, faith-filled prayers. That's why we have people praying for healing, but never really believing. They are wishing more than praying. The sad thing is, Christians have been taught that praying is pretty much like wishing, mainly because they are told falsely about what God wills for your life.

You see, when I pray for healing, I don't keep praying the same prayer over and over again. That would mean I didn't believe fully the first prayer I prayed was effective. My prayers turn into praise, because I am rejoicing in confidence that God, not only hears my prayers (**1 John 5:14**) but, answers our prayers when we ask in Jesus' name (**John 14:13, 14**)! This is what God's word says, right?

Yet, we so easily forget how much God loves us, leaving us to never going beyond our sickness or illness. We look to the gospel with religious eyes, trying to dissect it like it's rocket science, but we never approach God with a child-like faith. *"Truly I tell you, anyone who will not receive the kingdom of God like a little child will never enter it* **(Luke 18:17)**.*"* We need to get to that point where we approach God like a child approaches his father, with arms wide open, believing that he is good and wants the best for us. Sadly, most of us just ask for prayer out of religious exercise, but we had already made up our mind about whether or not we will have to live with this disease or illness the rest of our lives. Christ is the Good Physician. There is no disease He cannot heal; no sin He cannot remove; no trouble He cannot help. He is the Creator of Life, the Great Physician who has never yet failed to heal all the spiritual afflictions of every soul that has come unto Him in faith and in prayer.

I am reminded of the story about the woman with the issue of blood in **Mark 5**. For twelve years she had been bleeding, and no matter what she did, she couldn't get better. She had spent all her money, yet no doctor could fix her, in fact, it says that she grew worse. She had no hope, until she heard about Jesus. She had thought to herself, *"If I just touch his garments, I would be healed."* And as she pushed her way through the crowd, she got her chance to touch Jesus, and immediately her affliction left her! Jesus then turns around and asks, *"Who touched me?"* Now, you have to understand something here, there were hundreds of people crowded around Jesus, touching him from all sides, bumping in to him, and probably grabbing at him, yet, out of all of them, He felt this one touch. It says in verse 30 that Jesus felt power leave him. Are you guys getting this? What makes this woman so different from everyone else who was touching Jesus? It was her mountain moving faith that pulled the power of God out of Jesus, and caught His attention! Her faith literally moved God! And she was afraid because she thought she was going to get in trouble, but Jesus looked at her and said, "*Daughter, your faith has made you well. Go in peace, and be healed of your affliction.*" God is looking for a people who are willing to push through the crowds to get to Him, a people who have a faith that says, even if I just touch the tips of his clothes, I will be healed!

Oaks of Righteousness

"The Spirit of the Lord GOD is on Me, because the LORD has anointed Me to preach good news to the poor. He has sent Me to bind up the brokenhearted, to proclaim liberty to the captives and release from darkness to the prisoners, 2to proclaim the year of the LORD's favor and the day of our God's vengeance, to comfort all who mourn, to provide for those who grieve in Zion— to give them a crown of beauty for ashes, the oil of joy for mourning, and a garment of praise in place of a spirit despair. So oaks of righteousness, the planting of the LORD, that He may be glorified. They will rebuild the ancient ruins; restore the devastated; they will renew the ruined cities, the desolations of many generations." -**Isaiah 61:1-4**

One of the greatest scriptures to me that show the power of healing and redemption is in Isaiah 61 when the writer prophetically describes a time when Jesus will come and plant oaks of righteousness that will glorify the lord. Verse 1 is describing Jesus, who was anointed to preach the good news to the poor. He was anointed and sent to bind the brokenhearted, to bring freedom to those who were bound in darkness, to proclaim the year of the Lord's favor, to comfort all who mourn, to provide for those who grieve, to bestow upon them a crown of beauty for ashes, joy for mourning, and a garment of praise in exchange for their spirit of despair. Jesus came to restore us and redeem us from anything that is not of him, and in doing so, He will plant us and call us oaks of righteousness, glorifying the Lord by our restoration.

Let me tell you this right now, sickness, hurt, pain, despair, or anything of the curse does not glorify God. When His people are restored from death to life, that is when He is glorified. When families are mended and cancer is demolished, that is when He is glorified. When someone learns to forgive and their mourning is turned to joy, that is when He is truly glorified. Just because God can use destruction to heal us doesn't mean He was the source of that destruction, in fact, that just shows how amazing God is. He can take terrible situations, and if you trust in Him, He can bring beauty from ashes. Like I have said before, grace does not need suffering to exist in our lives, but let me tell you this, wherever there is pain and suffering, you better believe that grace will be there and overflowing, especially in our weakness. That is why the Bible tells us that His grace is sufficient and His power is made perfect in our weakness (**2 Corinthians 12:9**)

Verse 4 paints an even greater promise; those who are healed and redeemed, they will rebuild that which was destroyed. It tells us they will rebuild cities, those places that were destroyed. God is trying to paint us this picture of a people who have been restored, but it doesn't stop there, they will go out and began to restore people, began to restore their families, and begin to restore their cities!

God's promises and His miracles were never intended to stop with us, but to have a chain reaction that literally turns workplaces, schools, and cities upside down. This is one of the most beautiful pictures in the Bible. We have the most broken people, becoming the most stable, but they don't stop with their own personal stability. They don't sit there and say, "*I can now live my life,*" no, they stand up and say, "*I can now rebuild this city!*"

Here is my main point: we don't get the rebuilders unless we get the broken people healed. We keep crying out for our cities and our nations to be restored and rebuilt but most of the body of Christ doesn't even believe it's God's will to heal, and then we wonder why our cities are not being rebuilt. We need a people who are restored and filled with the Spirit, a people whose life is a reaction from relationship with the Father, not just a life based off of memorizing and rehearsing.

Healing isn't everything, it's honestly not. The condition of their soul is my greater concern, but I can't pass up the truth that also says healing is part of the salvation package. It's all over the Bible. When Jesus healed someone there were times when He said, *"The kingdom is at hand,"* so it's so evident that restoration is part of the kingdom. Communion, aka Passover, is evidence itself that Jesus forgave through the blood and restored (physical healing included) by the breaking of His body. Healing is such a large topic to write about because there is so much. One thing is for sure, God's will of healing is seen all over His word, especially in and through the ministry of our Lord and Savior, Jesus Christ, who is God's nature (**Hebrews 1:3**).

The restoration of others rests on our secret life

"And when they had come to the multitude, a man came to Him, kneeling down to Him and saying, 'Lord, have mercy on my son, for he is an epileptic and suffers severely; for he often falls into the fire and often into the water. So I brought him to Your disciples, but they could not cure him.'

Then Jesus answered and said, 'O faithless and perverse generation, how long shall I be with you? How long shall I bear with you? Bring him here to Me.' And Jesus rebuked the demon, and it came out of him; and the child was cured from that very hour.

Then the disciples came to Jesus privately and said, 'Why could we not cast it out?'
So Jesus said to them, 'Because of your unbelief; for assuredly, I say to you, if you have faith as a mustard seed,

*you will say to this mountain, 'move from here to there,'
and it will move; and nothing will be impossible for you.
However, this kind does not go out except by prayer and
fasting.'"*

Not many people like to hear this but we as Christians have
a HUGE responsibility when it comes to the restoration and
deliverance of those who come to us. Many Christians in
the church now days would have prayed for this boy or
tried to cast this demon out and, if it wouldn't have
happened, they would have just given up, saying, *"This
must be God's will,"* but as you read this story you start to
realize that this boy's healing was solely placed on the
disciple's secret place of prayer and fasting, and because
they lacked in this area, they were not able to cast this
demon out.

Now, I understand that healing can be held back due to the
actions of the recipients as well, but there are certain
principalities and strongholds that require a very deep and
diligent prayer life. This boy had demons that caused him
to convulse and literally throw himself into fire and water.
This was something on another level, which required a
prayer and fasting lifestyle on another level. How many
Christians do you know that consistently pray and fast?
Honestly, not many, which is why I believe there are so
many Christians still bound. The church as a whole has
capped out because we have neglected a deep, intimate, and
sacrificial prayer life. We have neglected the secret place
and because of that we have kept people bound. Can you
imagine where the church would be today if every single

Christian grasped the importance of this scripture? We would be at a place we could only ever dream of.

I am not here to condemn you, but to open your eyes to the truth. Religion, for years, has slowly taken the responsibility off us and thrown it completely on God, as if we do not have a say in whether or not someone gets healed, but we do! I honestly believe we have way more responsibility then we tend to think. *"Everything happens for a reason,"* yes, and sometimes things happen because of our laziness, our ignorance, and our tradition.

There is so much to healing. There are many things that can hinder someone receiving deliverance and healing, and there are many things that can encourage and attract it. We have to come to the point in our lives where we know God's will. When we know what He desires, then our confidence in healing will go beyond our feelings and into assurance. So let me ask you something: how is your prayer life? Are you fasting? Do you spend time praying in your secret place? And if not, then maybe that's why you have not experienced people getting healed and restored in your life. Maybe it's why you haven't seen yourself completely healed. It's time we start evaluating ourselves and understanding that the restoration of the masses very well could be resting on whether or not we have an intimate relationship with the Father behind the scenes.

"Fear imprisons, faith liberates; fear paralyzes, faith empowers; fear disheartens, faith encourages; fear sickens, faith heals; fear makes useless, faith makes serviceable."
                    -Harry Emerson Fosdick

FIVE

THE WAR FOR YOUR HEART

Intro

This was very interesting chapter to write about because I felt as if I was learning as I was writing, as if God was teaching me as I wrote down what He was telling me. The reason I felt God was wanting me to write about this was because, there is a lot of spiritual warfare going on in this world, and as I visit other churches and ministries, hear testimonies on social media, and encounter other Christians, I have come to the conclusion that many Christians are losing everyday battles with the enemy because we are not properly being taught warfare.

As I have said before and I will continue to say, we have people flooding the alters to be saved, which is amazing, but once converted, they still lose the same battles day after day, never really being set free from bondage. *"The War for Your Heart"* was written to prepare and equip you to guard your heart above all else, for it affects all that you are, and to pay attention to the warfare of your innermost being, for from it flows the wellspring of life. Our heart is so important to the well-being of our lives, yet we have convinced ourselves that it can take way more than what it can actually handle of the world. There is a war for your heart and its time we put aside our fear of the things of the spiritual realm and embrace God's power to overcome.

The real battle we face

One of the greatest revelations I ever received was about spiritual warfare. For many of us, when we think of spiritual warfare, we tend to think of fighting the devil, which is partially true. The devil is our adversary, our enemy, and over and over again in the scriptures it tells us to resist the devil, to stand against him, and know his plans. I do not want to take away from our battle with the enemy, but I want to present another war we battle every single day: the war against our hearts.

During a conference in Kansas City, at World Revival Church, I was challenged to look at warfare scriptures and examine how many times it talks about the devil and how many times it talks about overcoming our hearts and our minds. To be honest, before we can even come close to overcoming the enemy, we must overcome our selfish desires and our old self, because even though we are saved and forgiven, there is still a process of transforming our minds and hearts. It's an everyday battle. What makes it worse is that I am telling you to die to yourself in the age of self-love.

Like I said, the enemy is called our enemy for a reason, but before we can help others live a new life in Christ, we must first die to ourselves. It's a lot like the emergency procedures on a plane. I don't know if any of you have flown on a plane, but one of the procedures when it comes to the oxygen masks is that adults need to put their masks on before the children. The first time I heard that I was almost offended. I thought to myself, *"The children are the priority, right?"* But how many of you know that if the adult isn't taken care of first and passes out, no one will be able to help the child? It's the same way in our faith walk. In order to truly be able to help others, we need to have a grip on our own self-control first or our words are just empty.

So, what does that look like? The concept of *"dying to self"* is found throughout the New Testament. It's our true essence of the Christian life, in which we take up our cross and follow Christ. You all heard the term, *"born again,"* well, in order to be born again we must first die to our self; the old self (our sinner lifestyle) dies and the new self comes to life (**John 3:3-7**). Not only do we become new creations in Christ when we accept Jesus as Lord, and step into salvation, but we also continue dying to self as part of the process of sanctification. It's like a one-time thing but at the same time a lifelong process.

Jesus told us to take up our cross and follow Him in **Matthew 16:24-26**, *"Then Jesus told his disciples, "If anyone would come after me, let him deny himself and take up his cross and follow me. For whoever would save his life will lose it, but whoever loses his life for my sake will find it. For what will it profit a man if he gains the whole world and forfeits his soul? Or what shall a man give in return for his soul?"* For those of you who don't know, the cross is considered an instrument of death. Although, it's a beautiful thing, at the same time, Jesus' invitation is an invitation for us to pick up our instrument of death and carry it. In other words, He is saying that if any would follow Him, they must deny themselves, which means giving up their lives-spiritually, symbolically, and even physical, if necessary. It's a sacrifice, it truly is. I will explain more on the cost of our faith in Chapter 8.

Guard Your Heart

Proverbs 4:23 tells us to guard our hears above all else because everything we do flows from it. This is why I really want the world to know about this. We have many Christians preaching about how we need to stand up against the devil, yet they don't empower them to do so. It's like me telling you to go fight in this war, yet I never train you on how to fight or how to defend yourself. Before we can be effective, we have to fight the war of our heart.

Everything we do comes from the heart. **Luke 6:45** tells us that the good man brings good things out of the good stored up in his heart, and that the evil man brings evil things out of the evil stored up in his heart. It adds at the end, *"For out of the overflow of the heart the mouth speaks."* According to this scripture, what we have stored in our hearts will determine what we do in this life. In other words, it's easy to talk about living for God, but eventually, what's truly in your heart will ALWAYS manifest in the open. That's why you can usually tell where someone's heart is at by the words they are speaking.

Here's the hardcore truth: Satan will come and tempt us, but the outcome of whether we give in or not is determined by the condition of our heart. Fill your heart up with trash, and you will become spiritually sick and your spiritual immune system will be weak, making you susceptible to attacks of the enemy. If you fill your heart with the things of God, things that are good for your spirit, soul, and body, then when the devil comes, you will be able to withstand his attacks.

Do you see what I am trying to get at? The devil comes to steal, kill, and destroy (**John 10:10**), that's something you have no control over, he will always come. But you do have control over the victory, and it is determined by the state of your heart. Why else would the Holy Spirit inspire the writer of Proverbs to tell us to guard our hearts ABOVE ALL ELSE? That means our biggest battle we have is against our heart, or maybe I should say FOR our heart. Jeremiah even writes about the state of the heart before Christ, "*The heart is deceitful above all things and beyond cure. Who can understand it?* (**Jeremiah 17:9 NIV**)" Of course, with Jesus, our hearts can change, but there are reasons why over and over again in the Bible the writers talk about your heart, to guard it and, if not guarded, how evil it can be. I can't name all the scriptures but there are so many that talk about purifying the heart, cleansing the heart, how the heart can deceive, etc. I encourage you to look them up and keep your eyes open while reading.

"*CJ, why are you so adamant about having a sanctified heart?*" Because nothing matters unless your heart is in the right place. Let's take love for example. We can DO stuff all day, really nice stuff, but if our motives (that come from our heart) are not pure, then it means absolutely NOTHING (**1 Corinthians 13**)! Did you know you can live in the supernatural yet still live unholy? We have a generation being taught to lay hands on the sick and cast out devils, yet, they can't even keep their hands off their girlfriend/boyfriend. I have seen it firsthand. In fact, I have been a part of it.

There's a sad truth of the Bible that says one day many will stand before God and say, "*Lord, did I not prophesy in your name and in your name drive out demons and in your name perform many miracles?*" And God will respond, "*I NEVER KNEW YOU!* (**Matthew 7:22-23**) Young church leaders laying hands on people and they see healings, yet, their lives outside the church are barely up to code compared with holiness. And I am not knocking the healings, praise God, but before I could ever teach people about laying hands on people, there needs to be a true desire for them to live holy lives before God.

Before I would ever make someone a leader in my church, I need to fully know they have a pure heart. This is why I see the heart being our biggest battle. And in all honesty, this is part of the reason our churches have become hypocritical and lukewarm, because we have leaders putting other leaders in positions that they are not yet ready for. Yes, yes, and yes, GRACE, MERCY, and LOVE, but there's a reason why the Bible says a little yeast works through the whole batch of dough (**Galatians 5:9**). In other words, even a little opening for the devil can become a gaping hole, tainting the whole heart. The truth is, a pure heart will lead us into holy-living for God, and with holy-living comes holy outcome. Not just people being healed and people getting saved, but people becoming disciples and raising up other disciples.

I LOVE seeing people get saved, but I want to see it go beyond that. I want to see them reading their Bibles. I want to see them resisting temptation. I want to see them giving up things in their lives that pull them away from Jesus or distracts them from going deeper. I want to see them changing their words because they know that they must be set apart from the world, not talking just like them. I want to see people doing things out of a pure heart, not just because *"that's what Christians do,"* plus, sometimes we want to look like we are actually doing something for the Kingdom when people are watching. Some people will say, *"Do you even pray for people or do things?"* But they don't know that you are always blessing people and praying for people, you just don't post it all over Facebook and Instagram for the world to see. For me, living for God goes beyond attendance in the church and putting on a good Sunday show. I want to see men and women truly change and truly cry out for the lost, like truly CRY out for the lost. And it all starts with your heart.

Most importantly of all, I want to encourage you with some last instructions in this area. We all want to change the world. We all want to change the atmosphere of our jobs and our family, maybe even our churches. Many of us want to see people get healed and the lost saved, and the blind see. That's good, but in order to see the extreme, we will need to live extreme for God. We will need to fight the good fight of faith, we will need to sacrifice time, money, and effort to mature our spirits and allow Jesus to cleanse our hearts. Every day is a day to renew your mind and transform our hearts.

God looks at the heart

I want to make this very clear, if you did a heart check and found yourself lacking in certain areas, do not feel shameful. We all will fall many times in the process of maturity. I want to encourage you right now to work on the inner you in a time when everyone is so focused on the outer. When Samuel was choosing the future king to anoint, he looked at all of David's brothers and was going to pick one based off of their physical stature, but God reminded him in **1 Samuel 16:7**, "*Do not consider his appearance or his height, for I have rejected him. The Lord does not look at the things people look at. People look at the outward appearance, but the Lord looks at the heart.*" When I first read this, I thought this was awesome because my looks fail me at times. This might be a sad scripture for some because they have tried so hard to work on their outer Christian life but their inner-self is a wreck. I want you to know that there is a difference between falling while striving for God and falling and continually going back to your sin lifestyle. God sees your heart and knows that you can be a man or a woman after God's heart even after we mess up.

David was a man that failed multiple times. His life was up and down, from murdering a man because of fear, to praising the Lord without shame before thousands, yet no matter what happened, God considered David a man after his own heart (**Acts 13:22; 1 Samuel 13:14**). If your heart is to please Him, no matter how many times you fall, get back up and God will continue to see your pure heart before Him.

Walking with God, dancing with the devil

Why is it that we have leadership within the church that never want to talk about Jesus? There is a lifestyle that is growing within the body of believers where when we are at church we "put on" our ministry faces and talk our Christianese, but as soon as we leave the church walls, it's like we turn a switch off. I have been around Christians, pastors and leaders within the church, who literally act and talk completely different outside of church because, "We are not in ministry mode anymore." Inside of Church they were all about God and Jesus and holiness, but outside of the four walls it's almost like they flipped a switch as if ministry was only ever inside a building or as if there were two different lives being lived.

My wife and I became concerned for the amount of people who were praising God one minute and then praising Beyonce the next. My heart grew heavy as I began to see more and more Christians try to fill their lives with the things of God and also the things of this world, abusing grace and thinking there would be no repercussions to mixing the two. To make matters worse, I started seeing a shirt floating around that said, "*I love Jesus and trap music,*" curious about what it meant, I looked it up and found this meme that had quite a few million views. It said,

"*I love Jesus and trap music.*
I can quote Cardi B and Corinthians.
My heart, mind, and soul belongs to HIM, but I do cuss a little…
I'm somewhere between Proverbs 31 & Boosie
It's okay… you can be both, he didn't make us perfect he made us human."

I cringed when I read this. Some of you are like, "*I have no idea who any of those peeps are,*" and that is more than ok. All you need to know is that this meme is saying, "*I love Jesus but I also love the world,*" and to many this sounds ok. To many this is normal Christianity. So many Christians, and I used to be there, think it's perfectly fine and perfectly healthy to follow Jesus but still hold on to the things of this world. My question isn't so much, "*Is it ok?*" my question is, "*Is it possible to call Jesus as your Lord and Savior, yet still consume yourself with the things of this world?*"

Now, this is a true, man-made tradition that is growing very fast within the Christian community. There is a Christianity that is saying, "*You can have Jesus AND you can still live like you used to,*" but I am here to tell you that this is what the Bible describes to us as LUKEWARM CHRISTIANITY. You are neither hot nor cold, you are lukewarm, in between, straddling the fence, and double-minded. I am not trying to condemn anyone, but I am not going to let the fear of offending someone hinder me from delivering the Truth.

As I am reading this scripture began to flood my mind. This mindset right here is the very lukewarm Christianity that Jesus warns us about in the Bible. It's a lifestyle and a mindset that is convincing people that they are saved yet they are still on their way to hell! *"It's okay, you can be both, he didn't make us perfect, he made us human."* This right here... listen, you are human, but don't let that be your scape-goat. You may think you were born that way and that's how you are but the Bible tells us to be born AGAIN. I understand we mess up but we are called to be transformed! God does accept you where you are, but He still calls us to change into HIS image, not the world's.

What about **James 4:8** that says, *"Draw near to God and He will draw near to you. Cleanse your hands, you sinners; and purify your hearts, you double-minded."*? Or **Matthew 6:24**, *"No one can serve two masters; for either he will hate the one and love the other, or he will be devoted to one and despise the other. You cannot serve God and wealth."*? What about **1 John 2:15**, *"Do not love the world nor the things in the world If anyone loves the world, the love of the Father is not in him."*? What about **Psalm 12:2**, *"They speak falsehood to one another; With flattering lips and with a double heart they speak."* What about **James 3:11**, *"Can both fresh water and salt water flow from the same spring?"* Or what about **James 1:8** that talks about how the double-minded are unstable in ALL they do? What about

Luke 6:46 when Jesus asks, *"Why do you call me, 'LORD, LORD,' and do not do what I say?"*

Sometimes I feel like Elijah in **1 Kings 18:21** when he approached all the people and asked them the question I believe we all need to hear at one point in our lives, *"'How long will you hesitate between two opinions? If the LORD is God, follow Him; but if Baal, follow him.'" But the people did not answer him a word."* I feel like we can be an **Isaiah 29:13** people where it says, *"These people come near to me with their mouth and honor me with their lips, but their hearts are far from me. Their worship of me is based on merely human rules they have been taught."* And there it is, that last part that says that their worship, or in other words, the way they lived, is based merely on human rules and traditions they have been taught. When Christians are lukewarm, whether we see it or not, we are teaching the world how to be *"Christian."* And through our traditions, our casual living for God, and our lukewarm lifestyles, we are showing the world, *"Hey, this is Christianity and it's ok to love Jesus but also love the world."* The world is looking to us to see if what we live is truly life changing and most of the time they look at us and think, *"Why would I want that? They are just doing what we are doing but calling themselves better."* The truth is-- and like I keep saying, I don't want you to walk away from this book condemned, but feeling convicted and encouraged—if we truly loved God we would obey Him (**John 14:15**) and be 100% devoted to Him, and within that lifestyle we will be transformed into the image of Christ, drawing people into a life that truly sets free.

In **Matthew 23:25-28,** Jesus is speaking to the Pharisees and says, *"'Woe to you, scribes and Pharisees, hypocrites! For you clean the outside of the cup and of the dish, but inside they are full of robbery and self-indulgence. You blind Pharisee, first clean the inside of the cup and of the dish, so that the outside of it may become clean also. Woe to you, scribes and Pharisees, hypocrites! For you are like whitewashed tombs which on the outside appear beautiful, but inside they are full of dead men's bones and all uncleanness. So you, too, outwardly appear righteous to men, but inwardly you are full of hypocrisy and lawlessness. "'* I know we like to believe sometimes that Jesus was a feel-good-hippy and was all about rainbows and butterflies, but Jesus came to bring clarity, even if it meant being bold and loud. It comes down to this: there has to be a point in our walks where we truly lay down everything for Christ. We let go of unhealthy music, relationships, language, and anything else that doesn't look like Christ, and we began the journey of transforming our minds so that we can look like our Creator. And much like when Samuel spoke to all of Israel in **1 Samuel 7:3** and said, *" 'If you return to the LORD with all your heart, remove the foreign gods and the Ashtaroth from among you and direct your hearts to the LORD and serve Him alone; and He will deliver you from the hand of the Philistines.'"* God saying, *"If you would just come back to me with everything you had, laying down your idols, laying down your music and movies, laying down anything not of Me, and give me your heart and serve me, I will deliver you and make you into the best you, you only ever dreamed about."* It will be a process and yes you will not be perfect, but slowly those desires for the things of the world will fade and you will enter into a life that is truly better and more satisfying.

I heard someone say, *"We are in a loop. We want to be better and we want the world to be better yet we continue to support the very things that are poisoning our society. We want better mindsets, yet we support terrible music. We want a purer society yet, we keep watching and supporting pornography."* And yes, when we listen or watch certain things we are supporting them! When are we going to start being real and showing the world what true, unadulterated, uncompromising, faithful, and joyful Christianity is all about? Maybe if more of us were diligently reading our Bible and praying daily, we would begin to see a shift within the body of Christ.

War for the heart

As I was driving one day the Lord spoke to me, ***"Do you know why the enemy wars for your heart so fiercely?"*** I just kind of sat there and thought to myself, *"Not really."* ***"Because whoever controls your heart controls your destiny."*** He then began to prove it to me through scripture. You see, wherever your heart is, there your treasure will be (**Matthew 6:21**). **Luke 6:45** tells us, *"For out of the overflow of the heart, the mouth speaks."* In other words, whatever fills the heart influences the tongue, and **Proverbs 18:21** tells us that LIFE and DEATH are in the power of the tongue. **James 3:3-5** explains it like this, *"When we put bits into the mouths of horses to make them* *obey us, we can turn the whole animal. Or take ships as an example. Although they are so large and are driven by strong winds, they are steered by a very small rudder wherever the pilot wants to go. Likewise, the tongue is a small part of the body, but it makes great boasts. Consider what great forest is set on fire by a small spark.*" Captivate the HEART and you influence the TOUNGUE, influence the tongue and you control your DESTINY. The enemy wages war for your heart because, with one's heart, you can control where they go in this life.

I now have a better understanding of why God talks about our hearts so much. He says over and over again in His word to "*guard your heart above all els*e (**Proverbs 4:23**)," "*to have a pure hear*t (**Psalm 51:10**)," *to pray we have an undivided heart* (**Psalm 86:11**)," "*to seek Him with all our heart* (**Psalm 119:2**)," "*Trust in Him with all your heart* (**Proverbs 3:5**)," "*that God wants to give you a new heart* (**Ezekiel 36:26**)," "*to not let your heart be troubled* (**John 14:1**)," "*that the eyes of your heart be enlightened* (**Ephesians 1:18**)," "*to let the peace of Christ rule in your hearts* (**Colossians 3:5**)," "*to call on God with a pure heart* (**2 Timothy**)," "*to fix His word's on our hear*t (**Deuteronomy 11:18**)," "*to have a heart of wisdom* (**Proverbs 90:12**)," "*to not harden your heart* (**Psalm 95:8**)," "to hide His word in our heart (**Psalm 119:11**)," "*to keep your heart on the right path* (**Proverbs 23:19**)," "*to banish anxiety from your heart* (**Ecclesiastes 11:10**)," "*to place God like a seal over your heart* (**Song of Solomon 8:6**)," "*to wash the evil from your hear*t (**Jeremiah 4:14**)," and "*to not lose heart* (**2 Corinthians 4:1**)." These are just a few of the 90 scriptures about the heart.

I really want you to get this: what we fill our hearts with will eventually rule our lives. Sometimes it doesn't take a lot to know what a person is filling their hearts with, you just have to listen to what they say and how they say it. I am going to be real right now, some of you are losing the battles in your life because you have unhealthy hearts. It's not that you do not have fruit in your life, it's that the fruit you do have is rotten because your words do not line up with God's word and it's due to you filling your heart with trash and expecting God to just move and bless you.

What we watch and what we listen to goes into our hearts, and just as you fill a cup with water, it will overflow water. You are not going to fill a cup with water and it overflow with soda. No, it overflows with what you fill it with. Some of you are wondering why your prayers are not getting answered or why you are not seeing God manifest in your life and it's because your words suck. You are filling your heart with Netflix and Kardashians and wondering why you have no faith in God's power. You can't pour out what you are not filled with.

I am here today to tell you to watch what you are letting into your heart! Our future depends on it! The future of your family depends on it! Do not give up your heart so easily. Do not let the enemy taint your heart. Do not fall into the trap that, what you lay your eyes and ears on do not really matter because, if we are being honest, it is LIFE and

DEATH. Ahab, the wicked, unrighteous king, was taken out with a random arrow that hit him in the joint of the armor. If you don't know what the joint of an armor is, it is basically just an opening where the armor comes together. It is the weakest, most vulnerable area. Friends, the areas you do not guard are the areas where the enemy's fiery arrows will hit!

When are we truly going to start guarding our hearts? When are we going to start seeing a pure heart is so much more important than that song we just can't give up? When are we going to start seeing that a healthy relationship with God is so much more worth it than temporary fills from Netflix? When are we going to start seeing that a life of holiness is so much more freeing than that beer you just can't give up or that relationship you keep holding onto because you are afraid to be alone? It's time we start winning the war for our hearts.

"Nine-tenths of the difficulties are overcome when our hearts are ready to do the Lord's will, whatever it may be. When one is truly in this state, it is usually but a little way to acknowledge of what His will is." -George Mueller

"The Pharisees minded what God spoke, but not what He intended. They were busy in the outward work of the hand, but incurious of the affections and choice of the heart. So God was served in the letter, they did not much inquire into His purpose; and therefore they were curious to wash their hands, but cared not to purify their hearts." Jeremy Taylor

"We must alter our lives in order to alter our hearts, for it is impossible to live one way and pray another." -William Law

"We can create as magnificent an environment as we like, but unless we change the heart it's all a waste of time." John Hagee

"My dear Jesus, my Savior, is so deeply written in my heart, that I feel confident, that if my heart were to be cut open and chopped to pieces, the name of Jesus would be found written on every piece." -Assorted Authors

"To have God speak to the heart is a majestic experience, an experience that people may miss if they monopolize the conversation and never pause to hear God's responses." - Charles Stanley

"We must have the glory sink into us before it can be reflected from us. In deep inward beholding we must have Christ in our hearts that He may shine forth from our lives." - Alexander MacLaren

"And as the circumcised in the flesh, and not in the heart, have no part in God's good promises; even so they that be baptized in the flesh, and not in heart, have no part in Christ's blood." - William Tyndale

SIX

MINISTRY: GROWING UP IN CHRIST

Intro

As the younger generations are taking over ministries and creating their own, there has been such a shift within the church, some for good, but others have shifted to more of a business, modern, friendly-seeker setting that is labeled "grace," but functions more as a man-made, legalistic setting. What I mean by this is that we have grabbed on to a ministry that relies more on strategy and programs than it does the Holy Spirit. We are so busy trying to be relevant that we have let in sin and we tolerate it, in fear of offending. God's plan for ministry is to fill us up with more of Him than anything. We are God's method. The church seems to be looking for better methods, but I believe God is looking for better men and women.

I love the passion, but the Western Church needs wisdom more than anything in order to control the fire of passion, which often times can lead to being led by our emotions more than being led by God. In this chapter, I talk a lot about mindsets and priorities more than anything. I even go into detail about the absolute need for the five-fold ministry within the body of Christ. This is the good, the bad and the ugly of ministry, but also solutions to shift the Church back to the heart of why we do anything: Jesus Christ. It's time to break out of ministry tradition and routine, and come back to a place of true worship and honor for God.

I wasn't even considering putting a chapter just about ministry but, I felt on my heart that someone needed to hear this. I am not perfect and God knows I am not someone who is a professional on ministry. I have only been in ministry for 8 years, 4 different churches, each one uniquely different in age, vision, and size, but the things I have learned in those 8 years has blessed me so much. Sometimes we learned by mistake, other times we were led by the Holy Spirit, but either way we came out stronger in the end. Although I have seen some amazing things in ministry, I have also seen and experienced mindsets and ways that would make a mortician gag. I want us to examine our perfect example when it comes to ministry: Jesus Christ. He showed us what our priorities should be, what our secret life should look like, and that the one thing that caused His ministry to succeed: relationship.

The importance of the five-fold ministry

As I look back on my life, I am very pleased and blessed to be where I am today. I also know that there was a growing process to get where I am. A younger me would never be able to handle and older-me lifestyle right now. I would have given up so easily. I probably would have given in to sin, turned back, and ran to a more familiar, comfortable living. But that's life--we live, we experience things, we learn, and we grow. It's part of maturing. We start off as babies, we learn to crawl, then we learn to walk, then we learn to talk, and so on. And just like in the natural, we grow in the spiritual the same way. As Christians, we all start off as infants. We read, we pray, we worship, and as we grow deeper in the understanding of Christ, the way we talk, act, and think changes into the image of Him. **1 Corinthians 13:11** says it like this, *"When I was a child, I talked like a child, I thought like a child, I reasoned like a child. When I became a man, I put the ways of childhood behind me."* At least, that's how it should be. As I look around and study different ministries, I have noticed one area that has truly stunted the growth of the body of Christ--the lack of the five-fold ministry. Tradition has taught us for so long that we don't need the five-fold ministry, especially prophets. We have developed this one-man show, and all the responsibility and weight has been placed on the pastor. I whole-heatedly believe that if we were to embrace and properly train up individuals to step into their God-given gift, each church and each ministry would prosper, resulting in a full spectrum growth and maturing of the Body of Christ.

Ephesians 4 says, *"It was he (Jesus) who gave some to be apostles, some to be prophets, some to be evangelists, and some to be pastors and teachers..."* Why did Jesus give these five specific gifts to man? *"...to prepare God's people for works of service, so that the body of Christ may be BUILT UP until we all reach UNITY in the FAITH and in KOWLEDGE of the Son of God and BECOME MATURE, attaining to the WHOLE measure of the fullness* *of Christ.*" Now, I don't want to go into extreme depth with this because, I am actually working on starting another book called, "Growing Up in Christ," that talks about all of this and the maturing process.

I just want to paint a picture for you, that shows us the importance of the five-fold ministry. God created there to be five areas, the prophet, the evangelist, the apostle, the pastor and the teacher, for a specific and important reason; to 1) build up the body of Christ, 2) bring unity in our faith and our knowledge of Jesus, and 3) to become a mature, adult in Christ. Now, all this brings about a ministry that is mature in all areas, and according to verse 14, this maturing process, that comes from the building up of the five-fold ministry, results in a foundation in Christ that says we are, "*... no longer infants, tossed back and forth by the waves, and blown here and there by every wind of teaching and by the cunning and craftiness of men in their deceitful scheming.*" Do you see that? We have many ministries and churches out there right now, who are trying to function with only one, two, or three of the five-part ministry, resulting in buildings full of baby Christians who are not properly maturing, making them vulnerable to false teaching and the traditions of men!

Colossians 2:8 says, "*See to it that no one takes you captive through hollow and deceptive philosophy, which depends on human tradition and the basic principles of this world rather than on Christ.*" When we are truly being taught the full spectrum of ministry through each of the offices, we are building a foundation that is not easily captured and deceived. Although, philosophy and tradition may come along—ones that look almost identical to the message of Christ—we will know the difference because we are mature, having grown up, and continuously growing up, in Christ.

I can say this because I was one of those people that wanted to go into ministry so bad, but had no clear understanding of how important all the offices are. I got my idea of ministry from the one-man-show ministries. I thought the pastor did everything and the people just supported him. I just wanted that full-time pay to do the work of Christ. I think a result of this kind of ministry has been us, the body of Christ, not seeing real results, and because we do not see ourselves flourish, we began to put our trust in strategy rather than the Holy Spirit. This may even be why your ministry never seems like it grows past a certain point. You may need to look at whether or not your team is operating in all five offices. It may be time to start training people in their gifts and believing God that He will send those who are not only gifted, but called to be at your church.

I want us to understand that there are prophets and evangelists among your church. There are gifts given to us by God that are just waiting to be pulled out. It saddens me to think that there were Christians who have gone home to be with the Lord that never functioned in their gift because they were told, *"Prophesy isn't for today."* How sad it is to know that so many God-given gifts were never tapped into because of ignorance, fear, jealousy, and/or man-made traditions that said those died with the apostles? Or even those who have been spiritually used and abused within ministry, that has caused a burnout or some frustration.

There are no scriptures that hint that we are to function in any other way than the five-fold, so why do we believe we will fully prosper as a ministry outside the five-fold?

The ministry of Jesus, not tradition

Tradition and religion has taught us that in order to have a successful ministry, one's church must be at mega-church status. Let me be real with you, it doesn't matter what your church looks like from the outside, it doesn't matter how much money flows into your church, and it doesn't matter how many people you have. I have seen smaller churches do more for the Kingdom in a year than a mega-church ever did in five! I want to see a church's yearly goals go from how man tithers they can get to how many disciples they can make!

EM Bounds said in his book, "Power through Prayer," that, "*What the Church needs today is not more machinery or better, not new organizations or more and novel methods, but men whom the Holy ghost can us--men of prayer, men mighty in prayer. The Holy Ghost does not flow through methods, but through men. He does not come on machinery, but on men. He does not anoint plans, but men--men of prayer.*" Prayer is the fuel that drives your ministry, yet so many put it on the back burner, foolishly thinking that they can be successful without it. If anyone was an example of how important prayer was, it was Jesus. He was the Son of Man and the Son of God, yet the foundation of his ministry was prayer. He would constantly go off and pray to the Father. He had an understanding that his success was only as strong as His prayer life. If Jesus had to pray, what makes you think you don't have to as much? I remember a time when I thought my busyness was pleasing to God; as if, the more I was busy, the more God was pleased. There was one day when I was driving home, I kept thinking about all the things I had to do, and I found myself always offering God my service, which is good, but I felt in my heart that all He wanted from me was my fellowship. He desired me to do good works, but more than that, He wanted me to pray and to fellowship with Him. Jesus' ministry was founded on prayer and relationship, not purely works and busyness.

This caused me to really take a look at the ministry of Jesus to get a better glimpse of how the modern church has lost focus of how and why we do things. One of those areas was fasting. This hit home for me because our church leadership just finished a 21-day fast, and it revealed some things in me that were not pretty. Even though, this fast brought things to the surface that was painful, embarrassing, and frustrating, I had to look at it as an opportunity to better myself. Many Christians are afraid to move forward because they don't want their sins being exposed. In fact, there are even leaders within the church who continue to hide their sins and cover up their faults because they do not want to look weak. But in order to become a better you, we must address our issues when they surface, but not only address them and get rid of it, we have to fill those voids with the things of God once we do.

There was a time when somebody asked me to pray over this woman and cast out a demon. I begin to pace back and forth, asking God what I should do. He told me NO. The reason God had told me no was because, one must not only be delivered, but be willing to change their lifestyle— filling the gaps that were left open, with the things of God. If I were to cast out a demon by the name of Jesus and they never took the appropriate steps to change their lifestyle, then, as the Bible says in **Matthew 12**, *"When it (the demon) arrives, it finds the house unoccupied, swept clean and put in order. Then it goes and takes with it seven other spirits more wicked than itself, and they go in and live there. And the final condition of that person is worse than the first..."* I don't want to be responsible for making a situation like that worse, which is why it's so important to 1) be led by the Holy Spirit, and 2) fill the empty spaces in your life with God.

You see, Jesus wasn't demon possessed or anything, but one thing He did do through fasting and prayer, is that he emptied himself. He emptied himself and humbled himself, yielding to the Father's will and yielding to His love. The one thing I love about Jesus was His method of ministry. His ministry was so different from what many of us do today. He had no will of His own, He wanted to please the Father. He didn't want praise and didn't seek to impress people with who He was or how many followers he had. In fact, He loved people, but wasn't afraid to draw people away with the hard-to-swallow truth at times. He didn't rely on strategy or programs, He was in tune with the father, and allowed the power of God to flow through Him at all times. The thing that I find most beautiful about Jesus and His ministry, was the fact that He would stop and change His plans, just to minister to one person; for just one life. And even though He healed ALL who came to Him, He reminded us what true ministry is all about: people.

There were times when I forgot that. I was so caught up in *"ministry,"* that I forgot to minister. In fact, I was trying so hard to be that person who can fix anything and do everything, I forgot that my job is to minister, and God's job is to heal and restore. Paul David Tripp said it like this, *"Ministry is not about fixing everything in sight. Personal ministry is about connecting people with Christ so that they are able to think as he would have them think, desire what he says is best, and do what he calls them to do, even if their circumstances never get "fixed." It involves exposing hurt, lost, and confused people to God's glory, so that they give up their pursuit of their own glory and love for His."* We tend to forget that, although God desires to bless and restore us, His primary goal is not to always change our circumstances, situations, or even relationships, so that we can be happy. He wants to change us and mature us through our situations and relationships, so that we will become a holy people. I understand that, sometimes we get ourselves into situations, and it happens, but even though God didn't orchestrate that, He can still use it to grow us if we are willing to seek Him for help.

It always comes back to relationship. It's all about relationship, and although, doing work is a part of ministry, we have glorified busyness and have passed down the teaching that the busier we are, the better we are doing ministry. I will say this, as someone who sometimes forgets to just sit down and be present, beware of any work for

God that causes or allows you to lose focus on Him. There are plenty of Christians who worship their work. When we lack the controlling importance of concentration on God, it is so easy to become overly burdened and burnt out by His work. We then become slaves to our own limits, having no real freedom. Our spiritual immune system weakens and we become easily susceptible. That's when ministry becomes a burden more than a delight. Sadly, this is where I have seen so many ministries. We have been convinced that ministry can only be done within the four walls of the church. Tradition taught us ministry is only for those with a microphone. I would like to encourage you to stop limiting what real ministry is. We need to realize that your ministry is how much you tip when you go out to eat with friends or family. Ministry is the condition you leave a place in after an event or a trip. Your ministry is the way you love people; it's the way you love your wife and kids; it's the way you love your husband. Ministry is how you steward the love of Christ, and freely giving it out wherever you go. God is not just in the big things, He is in our simple deeds as well, we just need to learn to find Him there.

The next step

The more we mature, the more effective our ministries will be. And when I say ministries, I am not just talking about "*church*," I am talking about our marriages, friendships, and even our jobs. Like I said previously, many churches are filling up with younger leaders now days, and although we have the passion, we also need to increase our desire to mature in Christ Jesus. These next sections are areas we all, young or old, can grab a hold of. These are things I have learned over the years of ministry, and in fact, God has shown me a good chunk of these within the past year. I believe these are all amazing reminders that 1) we must seek wisdom at all times, 2) There is a process that we must learn to embrace, not run from, 3) we need to learn patience during the waiting. We may be behind the scenes for a while before God has us step out, but that's ok! 4) We need to start changing our prospective when it comes to the battles of this life, and 5) in order to mature and grow into a more accurate display of Jesus, we must learn to be faithful in the small things, putting our flesh down and not giving up so easily. These next five sections, I pray, will bless you and open your eyes to some of the things that every Christian and leader within the Church needs to hear, understand, and put into practice.

The passionate, plus the wise

God is using this young generation like no other, and although it's an amazing thing, I see great power needing stability. What I mean by that is that we need more role models stepping up and fathering and mothering the younger generation. Even though they are on fire and doing great exploits for the Kingdom, I see a need for a seriousness as well. Seeing God move gets me fired up, but there is a time and a place to joke around and be loud. I have seen leaders in the church joke around as if they were in high school, and the worst part was that there were new believers around desiring prayer and deliverance, yet it was difficult to do so because of the distractions. I love the excitement, I really do, but we need to also be aware of our surroundings and be sensitive to who we are in the presence of.

I still consider myself young, and even though I am currently 29, sometimes I feel like I am in my early 20'S. I love that youthfulness in me, but I also need wisdom of when to be goofy and fun, and when to be serious and firm. We get excited, and that's perfectly fine, but we must always be aware of our surroundings, being sensitive to the Holy Spirit.

I remember listening to Joyce Meyer talk about how the passion of the young Christians need to be combined with the wisdom of the older Christians in order to balance out this movement of God. She told a story about the first time she met Steven Furtick and how he sat down with her and just began to ask question after question, soaking in everything she had to say. I don't listen to much of Steven Furtick, but that right there is a humble and powerful thing to do. Honestly, It's something we all need to do. We as young men and women of God need to find someone with years of wisdom and experience to sit under and learn. I have been around a lot of young, on fire Christians, and although they are passionate, they lack a maturity that is balanced out when someone with wisdom is added to the mix.

Look at Peter, he was a man so zealous to please Jesus, yet over and over again he stumbled and seemed as though he had no control. Passion can only get you so far, and even though God is searching for a people who are on fire and hungry, he also desires for us to grow deep roots of maturity and stability. I think a big part of this wisdom we are needing is the wisdom and discernment of being slow to speak, quick to listen, and slow to anger. I'll show you what I mean.

Luke 9:28-36 tells a familiar story of Jesus on the mount of transfiguration. *"About eight days after Jesus said this, he took Peter, John and James with him and went up onto a mountain to pray. As he was praying, the appearance of his face changed, and his clothes became as bright as a flash of lightning. Two men, Moses and Elijah, appeared in glorious splendor, talking with Jesus. They spoke about his departure, which he was about to bring to fulfillment at Jerusalem. Peter and his companions were very sleepy, but when they became fully awake, they saw his glory and the two men standing with him. As the men were leaving Jesus, Peter said to him, "Master, it is good for us to be here. Let us put up three shelters—one for you, one for Moses and one for Elijah." (He did not know what he was saying.) While he was speaking, a cloud appeared and covered them, and they were afraid as they entered the cloud. A voice came from the cloud, saying, "This is my Son, whom I have chosen; listen to him." When the voice had spoken, they found that Jesus was alone. The disciples kept this to themselves and did not tell anyone at that time what they had seen.*

If you read closely, Peter is caught up in this amazing moment of glory, he gets excited and without really thinking (it literally says he didn't know what he was saying) he speaks up and is like, *"Hey Jesus, this is an amazing moment and I am glad we are here. Should we, like, build you guys a couple tents so you can hang out in there?"* He literally just started to say whatever came to his mind. Can we be honest here? How many times do we get caught up in God's glory and instead of embracing the moment, we feel the need to start talking or "prophesying?" We as young, passionate believers do this a lot. We get so pumped up we just want to post something or tweet something or take a picture, sometimes we are meant to just take it in and be blessed by the moment. We always seem to want to speak a word over someone. Someone with wisdom has showed me the importance of these moments. Do I still mess up in this area? Of course! I let my excitement get the best of me, and hey, sometimes God may be calling in those moments to step out and do something, but that's why it's important to be sensitive to the Spirit and know the *when* and *how*. If you are in leadership, do people actually take you seriously? Can a group of people look at you and think to themselves, *"Yea, I can stand behind them and know things will get done."*? How are we with other people? Do we joke too much? Are we sarcastic all the time? Are we always pranking people? Do people take you seriously? These are all questions I ask myself daily. I want to be that leader that people can get behind and feel secure in, not only my passion, but my maturity.

I don't want to discourage anyone thinking they can't jump around and be excited, seriously, it's much needed in the body of Christ, I am just saying we need to be careful that we are not out of control with it either.

The process

"BE PATIENT!" I am sure we have all heard that before. I have a feeling God says that a lot to His people. We have a tendency to want things now. It's hard waiting for success in a get-rich-quick world, but while some things may seem easy to obtain, God's plan for our lives requires us to be patient and trust the growing process. When I think of "trusting the process," I immediately think of David. He has a very interesting story, one that really changes your prospective about what it means to wait on God.

We first hear about David in **1 Samuel 16**. Samuel has come to anoint the next king of Israel and he will choose one of Jesse's sons. "*When they arrived, Samuel saw Eliab and thought, "Surely the Lord's anointed stands here before the Lord." But the Lord said to Samuel, "Do not consider his appearance or his height, for I have rejected him. The Lord does not look at the things man looks at. Man looks at the outward appearance, but the Lord looks at the heart.' Then Jesse called Abinadab and had him pass in front of Samuel. But Samuel said, 'The Lord has not chosen this one either.' Jesse had Shammah pass by, but Samuel said, "Nor has the Lord chosen this one,'* (**1 Samuel 16:6-9**). Eventually, 7 out of 8 sons of Jesse passed before Samuel, but the Lord had said no to all of them.

I want to encourage you for a second. Samuel took one good look the Eliab and thought, this man had to be God's anointed because of his looks and stature, but praise God we are not chosen by our appearances. This is what I love about God. We as humans tend to think that the better looking and the better dressed someone is, the more God can use them, but that is so far from the truth! You could have four years of bible college training, which is awesome, but that doesn't mean you have more anointing or a better chance at being used by God. In fact, I have seen God use former gangsters and prostitutes, who have no college degree and no bible training, just complete faith in God and a powerful testimony!

As I said in a previous chapter, God looks at your heart, which is good news for many of us! God has chosen the foolish things of this world to shame the wise, and I don't know about you but that is really good news for me because I was that foolish thing that He chose! I feel like many of us reading this right now doubt God's calling on our lives sometimes, because we feel like we are not meeting certain standards that men and women set before us. I want to tell you right now that God is not looking at what others are judging you by, God is looking at your heart! We have a lot of Christians who think that just because someone has a large Instagram following, has money, and is good at speaking, that God has anointed them and MUST be using them like crazy. I'm here to tell you to not worry about that stuff! As long as your heart is willing to please God, He can do mighty things through you!

And this is where we meet David. David wasn't even invited to the anointing ceremony! I am sure he was considered, "not qualified," according to the world, but every single one of Jesse's sons failed the test and when Samuel asked if these are all his sons, Jesse responds with, *"There is still the youngest, but he is tending the sheep."* Samuel had them send for him immediately! Friends, you may be in a place right now where you feel just like David, out of the picture and unqualified. But I want to tell you that before you are called into the light, God is approving you in private. This is hard for so many of us now days because we want the world to know that God is doing things through us. We post, we go live, we snap pictures of us praying for people, and there is nothing wrong with that, IF your heart is in the right place, but can I be honest and vulnerable with you? There were times in my life that I wanted to make sure people knew God was using me and that I had wisdom on things of the Bible, so I would post pictures or write a status. I remember times when I would meet new believers and I would be so insecure and intimidated that I would respond with spiritual things just so they knew I had a relationship with God. Sounds pathetic huh? But I wanted to Instagram my entire life so people would know! But here is the honest truth, if you truly do have a relationship with the Lord, and if you are truly anointed by God for certain purpose, you won't have to put it all on display, God will do that for you! He will make it happen in the perfect time! And don't think for one minute that just because you feel unnoticed that God is not using you because He is!

David was in the field doing his job when Samuel called

for him! David didn't have to sneak in and he didn't try and make a way for himself, he was just doing what he was first called to do and they sent for him! And here is the big kicker, even after David came and was anointed, did he go to the palace? No, in fact, he went back to the field to tend to the sheep! It must have been a big moment for him. This young man was literally being anointed to be king one day. He must have been overwhelmed, but just as quick as that moment came, it left, and David must have been like, "*Is this where I hitch a ride with you to the palace?*" But Samuel left and David went back to the pasture. The future King of Israel… in the pasture taking care of sheep. Yet that's where so many of us are at and we think that's our life forever.

Just because God has anointed you and placed promises in you, doesn't mean you will be positioned immediately. Some of us know God has called us, we know of dreams he has given us, and we know certain positions will be ours, but we automatically think we will be there the next day, but God is telling us that there are things that he needs to workout in us first. When I first knew I was called to teach and preach, I am not going to lie, I wanted the stage and the mic right away! I thought God was going to take me straight to the platform. I thought I was ready, but I was humbled really quick when God spoke to me and said, "*I do not want you to ask to speak anywhere. Do not send emails, do not post statuses, and do not drop hints that you want to speak at events or churches. If I want you to speak somewhere I will set it up for you.*" And so since then, I have never once asked to speak at any church, God has always had people send for me or ask for me. And if you go around asking to speak, then that's ok, that's between you and God, but this was a personal conviction for me because God knows my heart and He knew that the moment I started asking to preach at churches, would be the moment it stopped becoming about God and His people, and started becoming about my agenda.

In fact, God had spoken to me one day very boldly and said, "***My people need to stop building their ministries and start building my kingdom!***" And it's true! We try and make ourselves known, we try and force God's anointing and positioning, building our own ministries, but we never let God orchestrate our callings! David was anointed and I am sure he was probably like, "*Sweet, let's go to the palace and start this!*" But David didn't become king until years later! In fact, this anointing service wasn't even a public anointing service, it was privately done (the public anointing didn't happen until much later in **2 Samuel 2:4**; **5:3**). David was anointed to be the next king and no one knew about it! Most of us would be going Facebook live, titling it, "*God doing big things, I am so humbled. Palace, here I come #Blessed.*" But David went right back to the first thing God had called him to do—tending the sheep. God has called you, yes, but first He is telling you to go back and do the first thing he told you to do; be a blessing and influence where you are at! This may require you to go back to a place that maybe wasn't in your planner; a place that you never saw yourself at. It's probably a place that you don't even want to be! But trust the process!

I remember I had gotten saved and on fire for God, and a year later I moved to the city to live with my dad and go to college. I was there for four years and I remember telling God that I never would go back to that small town of 5,700 people (the place I got saved at). Guess what, God called me and sent me back to this small town and even sent Leana, my wife, from California all the way to this small town in Iowa! I was so upset! But at the end of our two-year season there, I am not going to lie, it was an amazing season.

It was in that place where God was working on me, pruning me, refining me, growing and molding me. He was preparing me because He saw what I needed in order to be where I am today. Two years I was there and then I spent two years in Georgia, which was a very hard season for Leana and I. God's promises seemed closer but at the same time, so far away. But God had a plan and there was a process I had to go through. It was my wilderness season!

God is wanting to know if we will be faithful in those seasons that create discomfort and pressure, so He knows we can handle the next levels in our life. It would be foolish of me to think that my promotion will come without the molding and refining of the process or without there being some labor involved. But that's the problem, we have so many Christians trying to rush the process in order to receive what God has for them, and most of them think they are ready.

Cornelius Lindsey said in his new book, *"Overlooked," "If you think waiting is hard then think about getting what you've hoped for and not being able to sustain it; that's torture!"* Wow, and it's so true! I couldn't imagine the pain of finally getting that job, or finally finding that godly woman or man, or getting to that place that you have always wanted to live in, but not being able to sustain it because you rushed the process and didn't give it time. Impatience is the number one dream killer. Impatience is a result of you letting fear stay when it shouldn't be allowed to live in your mind! Can you imagine David getting anointed and them jumping straight to the throne, no battle experience, no wisdom, and no testimony of what God had already brought him through? His confidence level would have been shot. Fear would have definitely run rampant in his mind. Failure and setback would have been his teacher. Let the process play out, be patient

Behind the scenes and in between

We live in a day where we always want the next best thing, even though there is nothing wrong with what we have! We want an increase in money from the Lord, but we don't even tithe and sow seeds with what we have. We want God to bless us with a new car, but we don't even do the basic maintenance on the car we have now! *"God, I want my wife now,"* or, *"God, bless me with a godly man!"* but God is saying, you are not even preparing yourself to be a husband/wife! There is a process of preparation we all need to do before the that thing He promised us may come to pass. God wants to work on us behind the scenes before we are called to be publicly displayed.

I feel like I have been behind the scenes for four and a half years now, and I am just now starting to see the certain plans play out. And let me say this right now, there is nothing wrong with the spotlight, it only becomes dangerous when we make ourselves the center of it. Stay humble, friends, because your humility will be your vehicle that will take you to new levels and amazing places. When the time is right, God will have people send for you.

You see, David was a man who could play the harp as well! And when Saul, the current king, was being tormented by evil spirits, David's name was thrown around that he could play the harp, and so they sent for him to come to the palace to play for Saul. His music soothed Saul's spirit and the torment would stop. You see that? Eventually they called for him, he made his way to the palace, and Saul liked him so much he was made Saul's armor-bearer. Give it time, men and women of God, be patient, don't stop believing the promise God has called you to, allow God to prune you and prepare you in private, so when the moment comes when you are sent for, you will be ready for the position. **Proverbs 3:5-6** says, *"Trust in the Lord with all our heart and lean not on your own understanding; in all your ways acknowledge him, and he will make your paths straight."*

I say all this because I want to prepare you. The enemy wants to blind you and lie to you about who you are and what God is calling you to. In fact, if you don't know the truth, then you will easily believe the lies. Michael Todd once said it this way in one of his sermons, *"There is nothing like the hit you don't see coming."* In other words, we must be prepared and ready because the enemy is going to come and try to destroy you, and if he can't destroy you then he will come and distract you. I have seen it so many times. I have watched friends, filled with God, slowly start making decisions based off emotions, before they realized, they were doing things on their own strength, accepting job offers that were not from God, moving to churches they were not supposed to be at, and trying to make the plans of God happen on their own, only prolonging the promise. Many of us think that Saul started off as a bad guy, but God anointed him to be king, and at first he was passionate about it and wanted to please God. Eventually he started to do things his own way, doing things "for God," but they were for his own gain. The enemy distracted him and eventually God took the anointing off him and gave it to David. That's actually when evil spirits started tormenting him. Soon, Saul became jealous of David and tried to murder him. He eventually fell by the sword and his legacy ruined. The enemy will attack you, discourage you, and attempt to distract you, but if you prepare yourself, then you can overcome them.

It's all about prospective

I Say all that to set up this next part, which is probably the more well-known story of David, which is the time he defeated Goliath. For forty days, every morning and evening, Goliath came out to the battle field and mocked God and Saul's army. And one day David was bringing lunch to his brothers when he heard Goliath talking trash. David was like, "*Excuse me? You talking trash about the*

One, True Living God?" David was all about God and wasn't about to let this uncircumcised Philistine talk smack about his Lord! He told Saul he would fight him but nobody believed in him because he was just, *"a young boy."* But David grabbed his sling, five smooth stones, and began his walk towards the giant. Goliath said to David, *"Am I a dog, that you come at me with sticks?"* And the Philistine cursed David by his gods. *"Come here,"* he said, *"and I'll give your flesh to the birds and the wild animals!"* David said to the Philistine, *"You come against me with sword and spear and javelin, but I come against you in the name of the Lord Almighty, the God of the armies of Israel, whom you have defied. This day the Lord will deliver you into my hands, and I'll strike you down and cut off your head. This very day I will give the carcasses of the Philistine army to the birds and the wild animals, and the whole world will know that there is a God in Israel. All those gathered here will know that it is not by sword or spear that the Lord saves; for the battle is the Lord's, and he will give all of you into our hands,"* (**1 Samuel 17:43-47**). You see, while everyone else was afraid and saw this moment as an obstacle, David, knowing God was with him, saw it as an opportunity to glorify the Lord. As thousands stepped back, David stepped forward. It's all about prospective! We always want to preach about the good things of Christianity; the promises and the blessings, which are true, but we need to start being real with people and telling them, *"Hey, storms are coming, battles are coming, and temptation is coming, BUT they are not obstacles, but opportunities! They are opportunities to grow, to mature, to prove yourself, and to glorify the God!"* **James 1:2-4** says it like this, *"Consider it pure joy, my brothers and sisters, whenever you face trials of many kinds, because you know that the testing of your faith produces perseverance. Let perseverance finish its work so that you may be mature and complete, not lacking anything."* When we are faced with "obstacles," we cannot cry and complain, and we cannot be of fear. We have to find the joy in it because when our faith is tested it produces perseverance, and perseverance brings maturity! Yes, we live in this cursed world, but Jesus told us that he overcame the world (**John 16:33**)!

Two things: One, Saul tried putting his own armor on David in **Samuel 17: 38-39**, but it didn't fit him, so he took it off and gathered his sling and stones. We are not called to be like anyone else. We may sometimes replicate certain characteristics, but God has a certain plan for you and if we are always comparing ourselves and trying to model every little thing after someone else, then we will not be able to battle effectively! Be yourself! Be that person God created you to be! Why? Because he created you with certain characteristics for a reason and those things will become the key ingredients to your destiny. David knew that the armor wasn't his thing, but what he did know, was that he got pretty good with a sling and a stone when he was guarding his sheep. In fact, he was pretty comfortable with battling large things because God had already prepared him back in the pasture! **1 Samuel 17: 36-37** tells us, "*Your servant has killed both the lion and the bear; this uncircumcised Philistine will be like one of them, because he has defied the armies of the living God. The Lord who rescued me from the paw of the lion and the paw of the bear will rescue me from the hand of this Philistine.*" You see, David was already prepared! He had fought off bears and lions who tried attacking his sheep. God had already been working on him in private so he could perform in public!

The second thing is this: It says in verse 48 that as the Philistine moved closer to meet him, David ran quickly towards him. When you make obstacles in to opportunities, run at it. Give it everything you have. It may not always be easy, sometimes it may even be scary, but know that God did not give you a spirit of fear, but of power, love, and sound mind **(2 Timothy 1:7)**. One day you are going to be telling your testimony to the world, how do you want it to sound? We can't be afraid of what the enemy is bringing against us because we have to remember who is with us and who is for us!

David walked away from that battle a new man and the whole world knew it. Those moments he spent in the privacy of that pasture finally paid off. The time he killed that bear and lion, he didn't tweet it or took a selfie and posted it, no, no one knew about his victories in private, and that was ok, because God was preparing him and working on him so that someday he will be approved in front of the world. But even then, that's not our goal. Our goal is to just live for God with everything we have. To love like him and talk like him and walk like him, and so when the position comes and when attention comes our way, we are so stable in him that those things don't phase us. Yea, it's nice to be noticed, but out identity is not in that. I come across so many men and women of God who want to be on stage and have a mic, and they feel like without those things they are not on the team. They come in, they don't even tithe, they only come to church half the time, and they expect the platform to be theirs. David could have cared less if the world knew him, he just wanted to please God, even if that meant working with the sheep and goats for the rest of his life.

David had a process to go through, and to be honest, that was just the beginning of it all. But through it all, even after he became king and even on his death bed, mistakes and all, God still looked at him and said David was a man after his own heart. **2 Chronicles 16:9** tells us that God is looking back and forth on the earth to strengthen a people whose hearts are fully committed to him. God isn't asking you to be perfect, he is desiring your heart to be fully his.

So you're called and anointed, that's awesome, but do not

forsake the process. Do not get discouraged if you haven't seen that promise manifest yet. Whether it's months or years, continue to do what God is calling you to do. Be faithful in those little moments, and take every obstacle that the enemy throws at you and turn it into an opportunity. That pasture your in is just a training ground before you reach the palace. And don't think for a second that you're not called and anointed just because no one sees you.

Faithful with little, faithful with much

Man, God has been dealing with me on this for the past year! I was, and at times still am, that guy who wanted more without even being faithful with what I currently have. We are a society that wants the large paycheck for doing very little. We start something new before we even finish the first thing God called us to. We call down God's favor and say, "*He will provide*," all while we waste our time, money, and effort on idle things and idle time. We say we don't have time and we don't have money, yet the truth is: we will always truly find the money and the time for the things we see as treasure.

I want to encourage you guys today, you may have to sacrifice a lot of time, you may have to say no to things way more than you want, but when God gives you more because He saw your faithfulness, well, that will be far worth it than those momentary fulfillments.

When it came to money, I always wanted to spend what I had. I remember being taught, that just because I have it, doesn't mean I have to spend it. It may take a year of hard labor, sacrificing coffee every day, maybe not going to the movies all the time, and I would have to learn to say no (self-discipline), but after that first year I would have money in the bank and things paid off. That sacrifice and hard work would eventually be totally worth it.

Some of us are in the same boat. God is calling us to big things, but that may require you to stay at your current job and work hard at it, despite being around worldly people. I understand jobs can have drama, and I get that you're frustrated and that it's not what you want to do for the rest of your life, but if you remain faithful in this for a short time, you won't have to be there for the rest of your life. In fact, the things you will learn in this current situation will be things that God needs you to be mature in, in order to reach those dreams He placed in you.

When I wrote my first book, I said no many times to hanging out because I had a goal and, in order for me to meet that goal, I had to put in the time weekly. I had to be disciplined. I had to pray and seek God and I couldn't let idle time distract me.

The other night I had a dream I was on a track, racing other runners. As I was running, I noticed there were hurdles in each lane but they were special hurdles, ones that required forty cents in order to pass the hurdle and move on. As I got closer to the hurdle I remember running around it while the other players stopped to pay their fees. I was in such a hurry to reach the finish line that I skipped right past the hurdle, thinking in my head that I would save time. I guess one of the rules was that if you skipped a hurdle you would have to go back to that hurdle, but instead of forty cents, there was a $40 penalty fee I had to pay before passing that hurdle. I remember the other racers passing me and moving on as I had to go back to that first hurdle. I could feel the frustration and fear build up. I woke up and I knew exactly what the Lord was trying to say.

Many times in our lives we are in such a hurry to reach our destination that we take shortcuts, thinking that we are saving time, money and effort, only to find out that it will cost us so much more. Have you ever had that happen? I remember when I first got my truck, I had went to the auto store to purchase oil and an oil filter, wanting to change my oil myself, even though I have never changed oil on an F150 before. The oil filter was in a tight spot that was very hard to reach. As I finally got it loose and replaced the filter, something didn't feel right, but I couldn't see the filter to examine it fully. Instead of taking it to a mechanic or researching more on it, I finished my oil change and began to drive up to the gas station across the street. All of the sudden I heard a loud pop and what sounded as if air leaking out of a tire. I immediately pulled over and looked under my truck. There was oil everywhere. When I say everywhere, I mean EVERYWHERE. I am talking about all over the bottom of my truck and all over the road for at least fifty yards back. I called my friend and we went back to the auto store where I bought another oil filter and some oil. This time I made sure it was right. As I sat there looking at all the oil on the concrete I thought to myself, *"If I would have just gone to the mechanic and got my oil changed, it would have cost me less and only took thirty minutes instead of three hours and twice as much money!"*

What I am trying to convey is this: there are no shortcuts to the place God is trying to place us at, because that destiny requires a maturing and growth. When a prophecy is spoken over our lives, the next step is not jumping into that position or place, not at all. The next step is the testing of our character. God wants to know whether or not we are truly ready to take hold of His promises. I see so many young Christians getting prophecy after prophecy of what God has in store for them, and they all could be very true, but instead of examining their heart and preparing themselves for the testing of their character, they begin making decisions as if that prophecy is coming tomorrow. Maybe it is, and maybe they are ready, but many times there is a process to reaching that place in your life.

I started doing woodwork on the side about 2 years ago. I knew God wanted me doing woodworking. I knew without a doubt, which is why when we first moved to California I began doing woodworking full time only to fall flat on my face. Where was all my business? Why wasn't I prospering? And as I asked God, *"I thought you told me I was going to have my own business,"* and God replied, *"I did, but you never sought me out on the WHEN."* And just like me, many of us are jumping on these prophecies without realizing that there is a process, a time, and a place for all of it. GOD WANTS TO SEE YOUR FAITHFULNESS. *"If you have not been trustworthy in handling worldly wealth, who will trust you with true riches* (**Luke 16:11**)?" If you are not being faithful with your job or your car or any of your possessions, then God is not going to entrust you with true riches! Sometimes you cannot be picky with your job, sometimes you may have to drive an old car before you get a new one.

One of the truths this generation needs to hear is that God wants us to work hard for our things. Yes, His blessings and favor is on our lives, but He wants to see us work faithfully at that job where they are rude to you. He wants to see us faithfully clean and maintenance our cars because he wants to see how we treat our investments. He wants to see how we WAIT for our next instructions. Are we just waiting and trying to do the absolute minimal? Or are we serving while we wait? Are we waking up early on our days off and getting stuff done? Are we utilizing our free time with faithfulness?

Not as we planned

Sometimes we think our dreams will come to pass in such a different way than how God intends. We, usually, think things will happen in a blink of an eye without any pruning or discipline. But I am reminded in **2 Kings 5** that sometimes our breakthrough, dreams, and healings may come in a different way than expected. Our story starts in verse 1.

"Now Naaman was commander of the army of the king of Aram. He was a great man in the sight of his master and highly regarded, because through him the LORD had given victory to Aram. He was a valiant soldier, but he had leprosy. Now bands of raiders from Aram had gone out and had taken captive a young girl from Israel, and she served Naaman's wife. She said to her mistress, "If only my master would see the prophet who is in Samaria! He would cure him of his leprosy." Naaman went to his master and told him what the girl from Israel had said. "By all means, go," the king of Aram replied. "I will send a letter to the king of Israel."

So Naaman left, taking with him ten talents of silver, six thousand shekels of gold and ten sets of clothing. The letter that he took to the king of Israel read: "With this letter I am sending my servant Naaman to you so that you may cure him of his leprosy." As soon as the king of Israel read the letter, he tore his robes and said, "Am I God? Can I kill and bring back to life? Why does this fellow send someone to me to be cured of his leprosy? See how he is trying to pick a quarrel with me!" When Elisha the man of God heard that the king of Israel had torn his robes, he sent him this message: "Why have you torn your robes? Have the man come to me and he will know that there is a prophet in Israel."

So Naaman went with his horses and chariots and stopped at the door of Elisha's house. Elisha sent a messenger to say to him, "Go, wash yourself seven times in the Jordan, and your flesh will be restored and you will be cleansed." But Naaman went away angry and said, "I thought that he would surely come out to me and stand and call on the name of the LORD his God, wave his hand over the spot and cure me of my leprosy. Are not Abana and Pharpar, the rivers of Damascus, better than all the waters of Israel? Couldn't I wash in them and be cleansed?"

So he turned and went off in a rage. Naaman's servants went to him and said, "My father, if the prophet had told you to do some great thing, would you not have done it? How much more, then, when he tells you, 'Wash and be cleansed'!" So he went down and dipped himself in the Jordan seven times, as the man of God had told him, and his flesh was restored and became clean like that of a young boy." (**2 Kings 5:1-14**)

Much like Naaman, we are expecting our breakthrough, or

in some cases, our dreams and calling, to happen in a way completely different than how God wants. Naaman was furious that his healing wasn't happening based off his timeline and his details. He actually had an exact way he thought it would go. It took his servant to remind him that God doesn't ALWAYS work in mysterious ways, sometimes, God just wants us to remain still and be faithful with where we are at. It builds character, it builds patience, and most importantly of all, it builds discipline.

We can't be a finicky people. We can't be all over the place. We have to be patient about where we are at and work our butts off as if we are working for the Lord. The process of walking into our calling isn't an overnight ordeal. There are people God wants to you to encounter on the way, people that God wants you to touch while you are positioned in certain places, and there are things that God wants to prune you of, but many times we don't let Him because we are so afraid we are going to miss our calling or that we are behind schedule.

I am finally seeing the harvest of things I have been praying for, for nearly 9 years now. I had to work at fast food restaurants and gas stations, I had to give up certain jobs, I had to live in places I didn't want to, and I had to work under complete jerks that were influenced by the enemy. But I knew that the things of God; those dreams and visions He placed in me, were rewards worth the labor. Was it always easy? Of course not, but I had tasted the things of God and I knew they were good and worth every minute of my sacrifice.

So let me ask you some things. Are you up and down, in and out of jobs? Are you always changing your mind about where you "think" God wants you? Is your YES a yes and your NO a no? Are you truly being faithful with where you are at? Are you taking care of your car as if it's a sports car? Are you keeping your house, apartment, or room clean? Are you organized and diligent with your money? Do you always find yourself not being able to give yet always being able to buy coffee or fast food? Do you feel entitled, believing that the things of God should come to you without any labor on your end?

I am asking these things not to condemn you, but to really make you think. I am right here with you. I have to constantly check myself all the time. But discipline, patience, and humility has been my platform that has catapulted me into the goodness of God, and it can do the same for you. I guarantee, once you start doing these small things, you will began to see the flood gates of heaven open and promotion come your way. God will began to use you in big ways and it all has to do with whether you are being faithful with the small things of life.

SEVEN

KEEPING MOMENTUM

Intro

It's one thing to get on fire for God, it's another to stay on fire. This chapter is dedicated to breaking down lukewarm and casual lifestyles, but also encouraging to build on those ruins, something fresh and new; a lifestyle that is completely sold-out for God. Throughout my life there has always been that temptation to settle in my walk with God, and to become casual with who He is and what He desires for my life. All around us there are traditions that have formed in the image of Christianity, but instead of sacrifice and dying to ourselves, it tells us that we can have all of God, all while still holding on to our past.

As my wife and I were transitioning from Georgia to California, God spoke to me one day and said, "*The way you end this season will be how you enter into the next. Keep the momentum and do not slow down.*" I took that to heart and we ended our season in Georgia full force for God, and we watched God turn our lives upside down in this new season in California.

My encouragement for you as you dive into this chapter: approach it with a soft heart, ready to receive whatever God has, but also, being ready to throw out tradition that has become part of your life. It's time to die to those things and come to life in the newness of the Father. It's time to build and keep that momentum.

Keeping your momentum

My amazing wife and I went to a *"Restore"* conference in April and it was amazing. It definitely restored a lot of things in our lives that had grown dim. It encouraged us, it strengthened us, it confirmed so much of what God has been showing us, and most importantly of all, it restored our momentum; that same excitement and zeal that we had at our early stages of Christianity. It was so refreshing and exciting. I felt like a new man. But as soon as I felt that fire, the Lord spoke to my heart very clearly, "***Do not lose this momentum***."

Many times in our lives we can go to an amazing conference, or maybe hear a sermon that fires you up, or maybe we end up going to church 3 or 4 times in a week and we get lit with the Holy Spirit to the point where we feel like nothing can stop us. Your momentum is strong and you feel like you are unstoppable, and praise God for those moments, but then something happens. In a week or so that fire starts to grow dim. Maybe that momentum begins to slow. What happened? Why? Why can't it just stay? What if I told you it can stay? What if I told you that you can live in those moments all the time? Yes, we may struggle and we may fall, but that doesn't mean we can't stop moving forward; that doesn't mean we can't fall forward, right?

I have learned something over the years: every day you are presented choices, choices that will either thrust you forward, like those turbo arrows on Mario kart, or choices that will wreck you and slow you down like red shells (I have Mario Kart on the mind). Imagine this: You just listened to the best sermon ever and you go home. You feel fired up so you think to yourself, *"I am pretty filled right now, I think I can relax and maybe watch this movie or listen to this music,"* but that movie or song does nothing to edify you or bring you closer to Jesus. There goes some of your momentum. You then have a choice to watch some YouTube videos or another sermon, you choose to surf the web for an hour or two. There goes some fire and more momentum. Instead of waking up early and praying, you decide to ride off the holy Spirit high a little longer and sleep in, there goes some more of that momentum.

Before you know it, you feel yourself slowing down. You thought you were so filled, that the things of this world would not affect you, but you deceived yourself. You took your free time for granted, and instead of going deeper, you stayed right where you were. You know what that really is? Complacency. You had opportunity to gain more, to go deeper, to expand yourself, yet you didn't because you were okay with where you were at. That's complacency. Deep down you want to go deeper and be better, but your flesh is convincing you to settle.

When I think of complacency, I think of the church in Laodicea. You read about Laodicea in **Revelation 3:14-22**. Probably one of the most famous churches of the seven that are in revelation, mostly known as the "Lukewarm church."

"I know your deeds, that they are neither cold no hot. I wish you were either one or the other! So, because you are lukewarm-neither not nor cold-I am about to spit you out of my mouth." (**Revelation 3:15-16 NIV**)

This letter to the church of Laodicea is the harshest of the seven letters to the churches in Asia Minor. By His indictment against their "deeds," Jesus makes it very clear that this is a dead church. Now, this doesn't mean there were not some on-fire Christians here who really loved the Lord, but that the church as a whole was spiritually uncommitted. Craig Groeschel in his book, "*The Christian Atheist*," Craig talks about how it's completely possible to be full time ministry, yet only a part time Christian. In other words, they were busy, they had deeds, but they were not growing. They were neither on fire for God nor were they unbelievers. They were pretty much Christians refusing to grow and go deeper. (I highly recommend reading this book!)

People will argue, "*It's not about deeds!*" And yes, good deeds will not save you, but someone who is saved WILL have good deeds in their life! Jesus frequently equates deed, or works, with a person's true spiritual state. He said in **Matthew 7:16-17**, "*By their fruit you will recognize them,*" and, "*Every good tree bears good fruit.*" Clearly the deeds of the Laodiceans were not in keeping with true salvation because the deeds of the true believer will be "hot," reflecting the spiritual passion of a life transformed.

I talk about all this right now because complacency is a disease that, if not dealt with immediately, can take you straight into a lukewarm and casual lifestyle for God. It's one of those things that you do not really notice at first but then BAM, you're in a place in life that you never thought you would be, or maybe a place you never thought you would return to. I really want you to know the effects of a lukewarm and casual lifestyle because, I'm going to be honest with you, IT'S NOT ABOUT YOU. Yes, you are important, but your faith directly effects those around you.

Here's a question: Why would God rather have you ALL for Him or ALL against Him? Because lukewarm deeds-those done without joy, without love, and without the fire of the Holy Spirit-do more harm to the watching world than the deeds done by those who are completely cold to the things of God!

When the world acts like the world, it's normal. The world is already the world! But when a Christian becomes complacent and lives a lukewarm lifestyle, then that is not a natural lifestyle of a Christian and it turns people off! I know I went from YouTube videos, movies, and music to harmful, lukewarm living, but it's a deadly process. One day you can be on fire, then a week or so of complacent living will push you right back down to where you started.

I don't know if you heard about the challenger explosion, but I remember hearing about the story for the first time and just thinking about how devastated everyone must have been. The space shuttle 'Challenger" just launched and then exploded during take-off. The first thing you think of is, *"What happened?"* After investigating, they pinpointed that the cause of the explosion was a failed O-ring seal in the right solid rocket booster at take-off. If you don't know how small an O-ring is, compared to a large space shuttle, it's relatively tiny.

It wasn't something huge, like a hole in the side of the ship, but a small, seemingly insignificant, O-ring failure. It was such a small part! But it reminded me of how our Christian walk can be a lot like the Challenger explosion. The small things matter, and if we let those small things go unchecked in our lives, our faith can end up exploding in our face. Our fire can be put out in an instant. Our salvation may be intact, but we will be no good for ourselves, our family, our friends, or anyone around us. Do not let things go unchecked in your life. Do not allow your free time to steal, kill, and destroy your momentum.

I don't want you leaving this chapter discouraged though, but encouraged. It's not too late! It's never too late. And God is a God of mercy and grace, but be careful not to abuse your freedom. Here is my last piece of advice to you: a good gardener not only attends to his garden, but guards it from any unwanted and harming creatures. As we grow and produce fruit, it doesn't end there, we must continue daily to protect and tend to our garden, to make sure we keep producing fruit and increasing in fruit.

Honor and Respect

My wife and I were youth pastors for a couple years in Georgia. As a youth pastor it is important to have visions and goals for your youth. Ultimately, every youth has the same goal: to train and equip young men and women to grow into the image of Christ. It's pretty simple and self-explanatory. But my pastor sat me down and really got me thinking one night. We were at a coffee shop and I was feeling very, well, I will be honest, lost, about my ability to lead a group of young men and women into the battlefield we call Christianity. He said to me, *"CJ, every youth has the same goal, but if you could pick one area for your youth to be known for, what would it be? Five, ten, or fifteen years down the road when these youths look back on what we taught them, what will they remember? What will be the one thing that we drilled into their lives over and over again, the one thing you want to stick with them throughout their lives?"*

Obviously, I just can't pick one. I mean, there are so many and we are called to be all, right? I chose the generic, "To be known for their love," response. He said ok. It wasn't a wrong answer because we are called to love God and love our neighbor, but it was lacking depth and meaning to me. I just said it just to say it.

Later that week I was talking with my wife, Leana, about what our pastor and I were talking about. She then gave me an answer that gave me peace and right then and there I knew that was our goal as a youth. Praise the Lord for wives, huh? I don't know where I would be without mine! Anyway, she said," *If our teens looked back on their lives and held on to one thing we taught them, I would want it to be HONOR and RESPECT for GOD.*" And there it was, the answer I was looking for.

Why HONOR and RESPECT? Because there are a lot of loving Christians out there who, well, do a lot of things for God, but their hearts are far from Him. They do nice things, they go out and feed the hungry, they attend church, lift their hands in worship, bow their heads in prayer, and say all these nice Christian things, but they only give God part of their lives. It seems like they are giving everything to God, but actions are lacking without a pure heart behind it; a heart that only desires to honor and respect God. They do not do those deeds to honor God, but mainly to check those good deeds off their Christian Checklist. And yes, this really happens.

I have met hundreds and hundreds of Christians who will not hesitate to tell everyone how they are a Christian and what church they go to, yet they are listening to worldly music, watching worldly shows, and talking in a worldly manner. That tells me that they are not firmly rooted in the Father. That tells me that they do not truly honor and respect the death and resurrection of Jesus Christ. That tells me that they have a lot of growing to do. In all honesty, it tells me they do not truly know their sonship. *"CJ, stop being so legalistic."* It's not legalism at all, it's responding to God's love with an extreme lifestyle for God! I am tired of people using "legalism" as an excuse to justify their lack of devotion to God. Our life should be a response to God's goodness in our lives. But not just in some areas that are obvious and convenient. I am talking about EVERY SINGLE AREA in your life. When we walk with God, obedience becomes a natural thing, but when we are not walking with Him, obedience becomes an annoyance.

I have grace and mercy for baby Christians who are learning how to live for God. Yes, they will make mistakes and they can still be in the process of giving up the things of their past and picking the things of God. I understand that and I am not talking about them. I am talking to those who should know better. I am talking about those who have been at this for a while. Because you know what, if those Christian veterans are not going all out for God after all these years, how do we expect baby Christians to take things seriously as well? How do you expect the world to want what we have if we don't even have what we claim?

I promise, I am not being mean, I am just not afraid to speak the truth. I would expect someone to be bold with me if I was living a double life or struggling with a sin area. The thing is, there is such a lack of honor and respect for God. And it's not just those who are constantly being caught in sin, it's those who keep tolerating it. Friends, we will not be judged by just our sin but the sin of others we let continue to live lukewarm lives and not do anything about it. Sometimes our messages need to be bold. Sometimes our message needs to be loud. Many may not like it, others may call you "harsh," but that's ok. The devil is out there like a roaring lion, looking for whom he may devour (**1 Peter 5:8**), which means we may have to speak up and shout over that roaring lion and his lies.

In **Leviticus 10**, God was speaking to Aaron and giving him detailed restrictions on how the priests should act. "*...this is a perpetual statute for the generations to come. You must distinguish between the holy and the common, between clean and unclean...*" This says to me that there are things that are holy; things that represent God and His kingdom, and things that are common; things that are of this world. Which one are you? Which one represents your life? Is your Christianity holy, or is it common? Is your life set apart?

THIS is why I want to teach our youth about honor and respect for God, because I want them to grow up and live a life completely sold out for God. I don't want their Christianity to be common, I want it to be holy. I don't want it to be relevant, I want it to be holy. I want them to be serious about their faith. I want them to live a holy and honorable life for God, not just when they feel like it, but in everything they do! If they want to go deeper, than they are going to take every free time they get to be praying or reading or listening to a sermon. I want them to not waste their time with idle time music or movies.

Let's be real here, the world thinks Christianity is a joke because of hypocrisy. I desire for my youth to not be less concerned with who they could offend, and more concerned about who they can inspire. Our youth are lacking because we have been terrible at training them up. If we desire the youth to preach the uncompromising truth in public, then we have to pray and pour into them in private. We can't expect them to figure it out themselves. And it's not our job to just tell them, we must demonstrate it. They are looking for Christians who are not hypocrites. They are tired of seeing people of influence living a double life. Compromise and complacency cannot be a part of a Christian's life. "*NO COMPROMISE is what the whole GOSPEL OF JESUS is all about...In Matthew 6:24 Jesus* says, 'For I tell you...No Man can serve Two Masters...' In a day when Believers seem to be trying to **PLEASE** Both the **WORLD** and the **LORD** (which is an Impossible thing), when people are Far more Concerned about Offending their **FRIENDS** than Offending GOD, there is only **ONE ANSWER... DENY YOURSELF, TAKE UP YOUR CROSS & FOLLOW HIM (JESUS)!**" –Keith Greene

A generation that lacks honor

A.W. Tozer stated this, "*What this country needs, what the Church needs, is the restoration of a vision of the Most High God!... There was a day when men believed in the sovereignty of God... The great God of the Bible is the God into whose presence you went with fear [awe]. You do not come dashing in wearing your tennis outfit... and then rush out again... The nearest Isaiah ever got... with God... was when he saw Him high and lifted up and cried out, 'O God, O God, I'm an unclean man.' When Daniel started to get [with God]... he fell down and the Lord had to raise him up. When John saw Him, he fell flat on his face... That's the God we want back... I pray... that the glory of God might be revealed again to this generation so that the Presence of God will be so overwhelming, so humiliating, so humbling, so wonderful, so glorious that... we will stand or kneel or fall down in the Presence of this Holy God and cry, "Holy, Holy, Holy is the Lord God Almighty."'*"

The church of today has shifted their focus from being all about the Father to all about our comfort, our ways, our needs, our ideas, our prosperity, and our problems. When will we ask the Lord for forgiveness and for Him to change our hearts? So many times we have asked him to heal and transform only for our own entertainment, so that we can have comfort and be blessed. All this so we can continue to follow the desires of our flesh. We treated God like a genie, and after he solves our problems, we go after our own dreams. I was reminded that we can sometimes act just like the prodigal son, asking for what was ours, but only to spend on wasteful living. We overlooked His eternal comfort for external, temporary fulfillment. The youth of today are wanting the real deal. I honestly believe they grew up in the church and left because they saw the hypocrisy of their parents, their grandparents, their aunts and their uncles and said, "We want nothing to do with your hypocrisy.

Frank DiPierto, writer of "Fire on the Altar," said, "*The Western Church today, instead of being different, is so caught up with worldly compromise, even the world is sickened by it*." And I couldn't agree more. The gap between being set apart and being worldly is slowly closing for Christians. We, as the Body of Christ, have justified so many addictions and lifestyles of our past and have invited them into our "new life" with Christ.

I just read an article the other day about a church in Santa Cruz building a brewery in their church stating that nothing in the Bible talks about drinking alcohol in moderation is a sin. The pastor even added at the end of his interview that his sermons are better after a couple of beers, anyway. I understand many will justify this and argue, and yes, the Bible may not flat out say that a little alcohol is bad, but it's not about a sin issue anymore, it's a heart issue! We are called to be set apart, living differently than the world. We are called, as kings and priests (that's what the Bible says we are in Christ), to set ourselves at a much higher standard than the world, not that we are better, but that the lifestyle of someone made in Christ's image, someone who is sanctified, and someone who is considered righteous, should be so different from our old selves! The first scripture I think of is **Ephesians 5:18** which says, "*Do not get drunk on wine, which leads to debauchery. Instead, be filled with the Spirit.*" And after reading his final statement that his sermons are better after a couple beers, I can only assume that this man is more under the influence of, "the buzz," than he is under the influence of the Holy Spirit. If you disagree, then go ahead and write me letters or inbox me. You can convince yourself that alcohol in moderation is ok, but, I will point out all the scriptures that tell us that it's not even about that. It's so much more than, "*is it ok?*" It's so much more than, "*How much can I drink before it becomes an addiction?*" It's so far beyond that, but most Christians just see through a foggy lens because their minds are not set on holy and righteous things, but set on how they can be a Christian AND still keep parts of their old life.

I am sure we can go back and forth about whether it's right or wrong, no one is going to go to hell over whether or not they have a beer here and there, but I must warn you, out of all the stories in the Bible, any story involved with alcohol (and I am talking strong drink, not wine because anyone who does research will see that the wine they drank in the Bible was very watered down) never ended well. Paul tells us that, *"Everything is permissible for me, but not all things are beneficial. Everything is permissible for me, but I will not be enslaved by anything [and brought under its power, allowing it to control me]* (**1 Corinthians 6:12**). Sure, it's permissible, you can, but just because you can doesn't always mean you should. At the end of my life, I want to be found as a man who took care of himself, who didn't give the enemy the smallest foothold. I want to stand before God and be seen as someone who didn't promote something that has caused the death of many, the destruction of families, and the destruction of the body. That is my personal conviction and I will stand on that.

The point of that whole rant was to say this, we are called to be set apart. We are called to be different. We have taken the holy, righteous things of God and have lowered its value down, making it casual. We have called good evil and evil good. It's time a generation of believers rises up and says, *"You know what, I am going to live holy, I am going talk holy, and I am going fill myself up with the things of God instead of satisfying my flesh! I don't care who I offend, I don't care if people call me judgmental, and I don't care if I don't fit in with other Christians. I am going to choose to be transformed into the image of God!"*

I am sure there are good intentions behind it. I feel as though this pastor isn't out to purposely make anyone stumble, and my biggest desire is to not create division out of a topic such as this, but as my friend, Mikey, reminded me, sometimes bad things happen out of good intentions. For example, in **2 Samuel 6**, David and his men are bringing the Ark back to Israel. They stumbled and the Ark began to fall. Uzzah reached out to grab it and he died. We can easily take one look at this and think, *"Wow, that is not fair at all. The dude was innocent!"* But there is a bigger picture to look at. Only the Levites were allowed to carry the Ark and David was not a descendant of the Levite tribe, and even though he had the best intentions, one of his men had perished because of it.

Another example I think of right away was when Saul was sent by god to attack the nation of Amalek, leaving no survivors, including their cattle and sheep. Saul did as the Lord had told him and attacked, but instead of leaving no survivors, he took a prisoner AND took the best cattle and sheep they had to sacrifice to God. God was upset with Saul for disobeying and sent Samuel to confront him. Saul tried to explain how he only spared the best cattle and sheep to sacrifice to God but Samuel replied, *"Tell me,"* Samuel said. *"Does the Lord really want sacrifices and offerings? No! He doesn't want your sacrifices. He wants you to obey him. Rebelling against God or disobeying him because you are proud is just as bad as worshiping idols or asking them for advice. You refused to do what God told you, so God has decided that you can't be king."*

Saul's life was a downhill spiral from there. He had good intentions to sacrifice to the Lord, but God desired his complete obedience over sacrifices. My point is this: just because you have good intentions, doesn't mean you are being led by the Holy Spirit. God is looking for your reverential fear way more than he is looking for your traditional, routine sacrifices. Some of us are trying to do "godly" things and we think that our business is pleasing to Him, but God is looking for your obedience. Maybe God is calling you to focus on one thing and stay still, but you think that the busier you are, the godlier you are. That's not true at all! God craves our obedience more than anything!

God is looking for the hungry

My church is currently experiencing revival. I know you probably hear that a lot, but hear me out. My church is encountering God in amazing ways; people are getting healed, they are getting set free from addictions, families are being restored, and individuals are giving their lives to Christ! The presence of God every service is breath-taking. Our worship is absolutely anointed and the fire and passion for God is only increasing. It's amazing and quite unlike anything I have seen before, but here is the truth I want to get by you. God didn't just draw our name out of a hat and was like, *"Congrats, Harvest Time Church in Covina, you won the Holy Spirit lottery! I will show up at your services and perform many miracles."* No, that's not how it works at any of the churches in this world that are experiencing a move of God. Can I be honest with you? The reason why God is moving is because there is a hunger, and it's not our emotions carrying us, we are literally crying out for people and hungry for more of God. We do not hunger just for our benefit, we want more of God because we want to see this city changed, this state changed, and this country awakened!

I have never seen a church more unified and passionate about the things of God. And one of the best parts about this church is the people, especially the leaders, strive to never reach a place of complacency and compromise in their daily walks. They are adamant about what they watch and what they listen to, knowing that we are either influenced by the things of God or influenced by the things of the devil. I see that and I understand why they do it, because that has been me and Leana's biggest conviction since we have been together.

We have been called extreme and even "overly spiritual," more times than I can count, but that's ok because, I know the convictions of the Holy Spirit in my life. While other Christians are ok with listening to worldly music, who they glorify just because of their talent yet, totally ignore their negative influence, Leana and I have never felt that attraction to indulge in that. We would rather spend our time edifying ourselves instead of filling our free time with idol time. I was going to mention a certain artist, but some of you may have been offended that I even mentioned them, but it's the truth, we tend to glorify people in the industry just because they are "gifted." I have been taught since the beginning of my relationship with God to be careful about what you let into your eyes and ears because they directly influence your soul and heart, and guess what, out of the overflow of the heart the mouth will speak. You will eventually imitate what you are filling your time up with. Your realm of influence is directly affected by who is influencing you. If I were to squeeze you, would Jesus come out or would the world? When people say things like, *"You are too spiritual,"* I always reply, *"Maybe you are not spiritual enough."*

I have witnessed a handful of churches never really grow due to poor leadership. And it's not that their leaders were terrible or not gifted, in fact, many of those leaders were very gifted in many areas, but I believe the real reason why there wasn't spiritual growth was because those leaders were not anointed. I will be honest with you here and I am not trying to shame any church, but we are really good at finding talented and gifted leaders, but we are not asking ourselves, "Is this person anointed for this job?" There is a big difference between gifting and anointing. A gift can fill a room and entertain a crowd. Someone gifted can stir people up and encourage, and all that is good, but it's the anointing that changes things. **Isaiah 10:27** says that breaks yokes and chains. It's the anointing that tears down strongholds and bondages. And as my pastor once said, *"The only way you get the anointing is by being crushed."* And it's so true, but we have a generation who want Christ and all His benefits, but they don't want to be crushed. Instead of being crushed by God (in a good way) they want to be glorified and the center of attention. They want to be paraded around.

When we have a generation of believers who do not desire to be crushed, then we end up with Christians who gifted but with no anointing. If this generation is never willing to go into the secret place and shove their nose in their carpet and allow God to mold them, correct them, prune them, discipline them, and teach them, then how will we ever change the world around us? How will we ever mature and be able to receive the anointing to complete our mission here on earth with great success!?

The place of compromise

It's crazy how history repeats itself. The things that happen in the Bible tend to go full circle, especially how the devil works. The Bible speaks truth when it tells us there is nothing new under the sun. The same temptations and the same battle that happened in the Old Testament, happened in the New Testament, and are happening now. For some, when we get saved we are on fire, growing and experiencing things at a rapid speed. It's not long until the devil comes around with a big blow to knock you back on your butt. There is no hit like the one you don't see coming. That's the hit that truly knocks you out, which is why I believe the Bible tells us over and over again to be alert, to be sober-minded, and to always be ready in season and out of season (**1 Peter 5:8; 2 Timothy 4:2**).

The enemy is literally prowling around us like a roaring lion (**1 Peter 5:8**), looking to whom he may devour, and if you have ever watched animal planet, then you know that lions usually go after the slowest, the weakest, or the most ignorant. Men and women, we cannot be any of these three. The moment we let our guard down is the moment the enemy gets his foot in the door, and if you are unaware of his presence, then he will eventually sneak in and do whatever it takes to steal, kill and destroy you (**John 10:10**). No one wakes up in the morning and says, "*You know what, I think I will fall away from God today.*" No, it doesn't happen like that. Christians are in a lukewarm and casual, backslidden life because, they repeatedly made bad choices that opened the door for the enemy. It usually isn't one big mistake, it's a series of small moments of complacency that takes us to a stagnant lifestyle. When we let thoughts stay in our mind that are not of God, we began to dwell on them instead of speaking to them to GO. Eventually those thoughts turn into words, and our words will turn into action. We think to ourselves that listening to worldly music is alright, or we convince ourselves that watching perverted filth on TV is not that big of a deal, so we continue to fill our hearts and mind with that junk, but then we are confused when we are still addicted to pornography, or our marriage is not healing, and our life is stagnant. It's because you keep filling your cup with moments of complacency and compromise, and pretty soon your cup will overflow.

Taking risks and playing it safe

If there is one thing I have learned about revival, it's that you have to continually take risks. As a man who is a perfectionist, this is my greatest strength but also my greatest weakness. This makes it hard for me to step out because of the lack of vision I see past my current situation. I remember I used to play this pool game on my phone. I would play it all the time. Every time you win you get money and the more money you have, the more things you can buy, and the more you can wager. My goal has always been to reach a million dollars. One day I played a mini game and I ended up winning $250,000! I was pumped because that is a good chunk of change for me. As I began to wager money and try to increase my pay, I found myself only playing small wager games, in fear of taking the chance and betting big money. Yea, I was winning but I was only collecting $5,000-$10,000 at a time. That's when God spoke to me. One awesome thing about our God is that He will speak to you in the least likely ways. I was playing a pool game on my phone when he spoke to me! Anyway, God said to me, "*You will never reach your dreams by taking small chances and making little sacrifices.*" I was floored. I knew it was true for my life. God has placed huge dreams in me and I knew it, but deep down I wanted it all to come without me having to take big risks. In order to truly experience God's goodness and be used by Him, we have to be willing to get uncomfortable. This is why many fall away because they would rather be comfortable and just getting by than uncomfortable and flourishing.

I'll be honest with you; true Christianity is uncomfortable. If we desire to be truly used by God, then we have to prepare ourselves to get out of our comfort zones. Many of us are like me playing this game; we want to go to the next level, we want to win the Jesus lottery, but we are making small sacrifices, which if we really look at the big picture, we are not really sacrificing, because a sacrifice is something that hurts to give up. We sometimes give God our leftovers and think we are doing Him a favor. We throw in a $20 in the offering plate thinking we are sacrificing but we spend more than $20 on Starbucks in A week sometimes! A sacrifice and a risk is something that will make us uncomfortable and is bigger than who we are. Like I said, I am preaching to myself. I have battled this for as long as I can remember, and although I am not where I used to be, I am not close to where I want to be.

Fast forward a couple months and I am at work in the warehouse. I am need of cutting a strap off a pallet so I ask one of my coworkers if I can borrow their box knife. They hand me one and it's one that you have to slide the button up, but it springs back in if you let go. It's nice, but it gets annoying after a while because you have to keep your thumb on the button, which was making cutting the straps harder. I return the knife to my coworker and told him that this is the coolest yet most annoying knife I have ever used. He laughed and said, *"You should have seen the blade that came with it. It was round, making cutting anything impossible."* I laughed it off and replied, *"This knife is so safe that it's unusable."* I began to walk away laughing until the Holy Spirit floored me again with, ***"Sometimes, my people are so safe they are unusable."*** I was straight-faced because it was true but also because I knew that was about me as well. When we are so safe that we are too afraid to make big leaps, we literally stop God from using us.

Jesus asked a HUGE question in Luke 18 that makes you think how important it is to have faith; *"When the Son of man comes, will he find faith?"* That's the question of a lifetime, huh? When God scans the earth and when Jesus comes back, is he going to find a people of faith? Will he find a people who were willing to risk it all and step out in confidence? I believe God is looking for a people that have no fear and no shame that are willing to make risky decisions and huge sacrifices. I don't know about you, but I want to get to a place where, when a crazy situation comes in my life, I don't even flinch because I know God has my back no matter what! A random bill comes in the mail and it's a huge chunk of change, I just turn to God, lift it in the air and praise Him that it will be taken care of. Or a sickness comes and attacks me, I turn to God and believe what His word says about healing, not letting fear creep in at all! Or I lose my job, but instead of being afraid, I start to dance and praise God because He loves me and He ALWAYS provides and is FAITHFUL.

Maybe God is telling you to start a business and all you can think about is what you have, or maybe what you lack, but let me tell you something, it's not about what you have that will determine your outcome, it's about WHO you have. God can take the smallest things in your life and use them to create your dream. Look at the widow who encountered Elisha in **2 Kings 4**. This woman was going through a rough time. She just lost her husband and men were coming to take her children in order to settle a debt they were left with. I am sure she didn't know what she was going to do! But here comes Elisha, a man of God, and asks her in verse 2, *"What shall I do for you? Tell me; what have you in the house?"* Elisha asked her what she wanted from him, but then doesn't even let her finish and goes into asking what she has. She replied, *"Your servant has nothing in the house except a jar of oil* (ESV)" When asked what she wanted from the man of God, she told him all that she had, and to her it didn't look like enough to do anything. All she had was a jar with a little bit of oil in it. But if there is one thing I know about our God is that he can take what the world deems "not enough" and make it into more than enough! She went out, gathered vessels, and began to pour her jar into the others, and guess what, it continued to pour oil until ALL the vessels she had were filled! Stop basing your future off of your current inventory and start basing it off of the God you serve and how much he loves you!

There is so much in this story, but one thing that caught my eye as I am writing this is the fact that Elisha made her go gather other vessels. In order for the oil to multiply, she had to find vessels that they could go in. God may have a dream for you with a supernatural way to get there, but it will require you to do some work as well! I don't know what that may be for you, but for me, I know God has placed a dream in my heart to one day have my own woodworking shop, but it's not just gonna fall on my lap. I may have to go out and get wood, maybe take some small steps to get things going, but God will place the supernatural on my obedience! I just have to step out, in faith, and know that God will provide the rest, guide me, show me favor, bring in the customers, and sustain me! But one thing I have to always remember is that if I want to be successful I have to take risks and sacrifice. Are you ready to get uncomfortable? Are you willing to take risks? Will you make the sacrifice? I believe most of us know what we have to do, we just need to step out and do it!

My promotion dream

In June I had a dream that I was working in this huge warehouse and I had worked my way up to becoming the best employee there. The manager approached me one day and told me he was letting me go. In shock I asked him, *"Why me? Am I not your best worker?"* He said, *"That is why I am letting you go. Out of all the guys that work here, you are the only one that could easily find another job. These other men, if I let them go, would never find work."* I felt bamboozled. The whole situation felt so unfair. I woke up really confused but then went back to bed only to continue to have that same dream over and over. I began to pray what the meaning of this dream meant, I even went to my pastor (who has a gift of interpreting dreams) who began to break some things down for me. You see, God is seeking men and women He can use, who are willing to step out and go places. These other men in my dream were ok with where they were at. They weren't putting in the work that would highlight them, which is why they were going to stay right where they were. As for me, I was the best worker there and, like my dream boss said, it would be easy for me to find another place, even better. As I began to dwell on this dream, God showed me that sometimes in our life when God wants to expand us and promote us, our process to greater sometimes looks like demotion to us. Yea, I was losing my job, but it was because there was better out there for me. Some of you who are reading this right now are going through what seems like hell, but let me tell you this, it may be a process so that you can have bigger and better. Don't give up, don't have a pity party, and do not stop seeking God through it all. Trust in Him with ALL of your heart, and lean not on your own understanding. He will make your path straight if you do not lose focus of pleasing Him (Read **Proverbs 3**). The process may never seem like what you pictured in your mind, but it's always worth it when you see it through.

I remember I would watch my grandma take a plant, pull it out of its pot, and then place it into a bigger pot. She would go about doing this about 3-4 times (depending on the plant) until it was to the point the plant had reached its adult life. I asked her one day, *"Why do you keep pulling those plants out and re-planting? Isn't that bad for them?"* She then explained to me that it is a requirement if you desire the plant to flourish and grow full size. You see, when plants outgrow their pot, they needed to be pulled out and replanted so they can continue to expand. If you were to leave them in a small pot and never upgrade them they will eventually die. God brought this to my remembrance when I was praying about this dream. In order for us to grow, mature and expand, we must be pulled out of our surroundings—the place where we have outgrown—and we must be exposed and become uncomfortable, and we must be promoted to a place that will allow us to continue to grow and expand our roots. It's a part of growing up in Christ.

Some people fear change so much that they stay where they are, never growing in their faith, and soon enough they spiritually die, resulting in a backslidden and lukewarm lifestyle. You may be asking, why can't you just plant a small plant in a large pot so you never have to transplant them again? That is a good question and my grandma explained it to me like this: if the pot is too large, the ratio of plant roots to soil will be too great for the roots to absorb all the moisture after watering, which leads to water sitting at the bottom of the pot and causes the roots to rot. In other words, the large area is too much for the plant to sustain its growth. Much like these plants, we ourselves desire to be in that large, promoted place in our lives, yet if we were to take on that place before we were ready we wouldn't be able to sustain it. This is why God has us go through a process, because he wants us to be able to handle those dreams he has placed in us. He wants us to reach that place in our lives where our dreams can happen and flourish. I have seen way too many Christians get saved, desire a microphone, pulpit, or position, and when people just give it to them they fall on their face, causing themselves to let shame and pride consume them. Desiring those things isn't necessarily bad, but if you are placed in a position like that before you are truly matured in Christ, it won't be a dream come true for you, it will actually become your nightmare, full of disappointments. We cannot rush the process!

And just a little warning for those who are being promoted, when God pulls you out of your "pot" and gets ready to transplant you, you become exposed; no longer hidden in a crowd, but lifted above the rest. Imagine there are five plants and you pull one up, what happens? That one plant being transplanted is noticed more than the others. Guess what? The enemy will notice you and immediately come to mess with you because you are exposed and uncomfortable. Prepare for battle, friends. Do not fear because God has you, but still prepare for some attacks. The worse thing we can tell people once they get saved is that life will get easier. Yes, God has amazing plans for us, He wants to heal us, He wants to bless us, He wants to teach us, but being a Christian isn't always easy. There are battles and trials. There are tribulations and some bad days. But that doesn't mean it's not worth it.

Have I gone through some stuff? You bet. Have I had some bad days and even bad weeks? For sure! Have I had some faith battles where I wasn't sure how a bill was gonna be paid? More than once! But God delivered me every time. And even though it was hard in those moments, it was completely worth it in the end when I chose to trust in God and run to Him.

I am here today to tell you this: Promotion is on the other side of your faithfulness in lowly situations. There are many of us who want God's promotion and expansion in our lives without ever having to do anything. We have some trust-fund Christians in here. We want to win the Jesus lottery and live happily ever after. Men and women of God, there are moments in your life when you will be faced with decisions that just don't seem significant in your Christian walk, but God is seeing how you deal with the small instances of faithfulness, especially when no one is looking. In 2013 I was an EMT for a private ambulance service in Omaha, NE. I also worked in the ER as an ER Tech Council Bluffs, IA. My schedule was great and I was making great money, but then God promoted me. At the time it didn't seem like promotion at all. He had called me to move back to Clarinda, IA, a small town with only 5,700 people. This is the town I went to middle school and high school in, the place where I encountered God for the very first time. And although it held fond memories, I told myself I never wanted to return. As I packed my bags and left I found myself three weeks in and still not being able to find a job. None of the hospitals were hiring and every fire department in the surrounding areas were all volunteer. I was running out of money fast and so I got a job at a gas station making pizza. Let's just say my pride was hit hard. I remember hiding in the freezer when I would see people I went to school with come in. it was an all-time low for me.

One day God spoke to me and said, *"I cannot give you greater if you are not going to be faithful with little."* I was convicted to the max. Here I am, working at this gas station, making pizza in this small town, yet to me, I felt like I was too good for this. I had to really humble myself from that point on. I changed my attitude and my entire prospective that day. I came into work with a smile, making people laugh, and working my butt off. I would see old classmates and wave and ask them how they were. It was actually pretty fun working there. I loved the people, I loved the atmosphere, and I was able to talk about Jesus freely. Even though my prospective changed, my bank account was also changing but not the good kind.

Even though I was working full time, I was getting paid about 1/3 of what I was in the city. I remember I had like $100 left in my bank account but I needed it for a bill. I was so hungry but did not have any money to buy food. I know what you're thinking, *"CJ, you worked in a kitchen!"* I did but one of the rules was that when the food expired, whether it was still good or not, we had to throw it out and if we ate any of it, it was considered stealing. Everyone would continue to eat it all the time, but I felt the Lord reminding me to be faithful, even in these small moments that don't really seem like that big of a deal. I am not going to lie, it was hard. I was hungry, I had no money, and to top it off, my coworkers would be eating in front of me all the time, but I continued to push through knowing that that God honors those who honor Him (**1 Samuel 2:30**). This went on for about two months until one day I received a phone call from a company who said my name was passed around and that they wanted me to come in for an interview. I went in on a Friday and started working that following Monday. This job was amazing. I was getting paid more than I was as an EMT, I was getting paid weekly, the benefits and commission was amazing, and the hours were perfect. I look back on that time in my life and I am so thankful I chose to never compromise. The things that God has for us may require sacrifice, but it's always worth it in the long run.

People look at stories like this and think that we are extreme. The sad truth is that so many Christians think of these things as small, no big deal, and petty. We have all heard it, *"There's nothing wrong with a little white lie, God understands, etc."* And the truth is this: small lies are still lies and stealing food or robbing a bank, it's steal considered theft in God's eyes and it's not of God's character so why entertain it? Why let that become part of who you are? Because the fact of the matter is that those small compromises will eventually turn into big issues if we leave it unaddressed. Look at the Old Testament at all the family issues they had. Father's sleeping with daughters, lying to spouses, selling brothers into slavery, the list goes on and it's because those issues were never addressed and solved, so history kept repeating it's self until the strongholds of the enemy were broken! You may think that I was extreme when it came to taking food that was expired, but God is searching for a people who are obedient, not just some times, but in every area.

Not too long ago my wife and I were applying to rent a house. We had applied to probably five houses and kept getting denied. I was so tired of hearing people say no. I began to be convicted because I had lied on the application saying we only had one dog instead of two, for fear of being charged double. I ignored it at first but then my wife came to me and said she felt convicted as well. I knew right then and there that I had fallen into the trap of compromise again, and if I continued to ignore it I would soon regret it. I called my leasing agent and told her to add our other dog on there and she did. We applied for another house the next day, a house that I really liked, and the very next day we got a phone call saying we got accepted for it. The Lord had spoken to me again, *"**I honor those who honor me**."*

In my honest opinion, it may be hard to tell the truth at times, but no matter the consequence of your actions, a clean conscience is far more rewarding then getting away with something with a lie. So many problems would have been avoided in the bible if people would have just told the truth. Adam and Eve blamed each other instead of confessing their mistakes, Abraham lied about Sarah being his wife and it almost cursed someone, Sarah lied to God about laughing at the idea of having a child, Jacob lies to

Isaac (**Genesis 27:19**), and even in the New Testament when Saphira and Ananias lie to Peter and the Holy Spirit. So many more examples of people lying because fear convinced them of a certain outcome. We lie to try and protect ourselves and it, in fact, only opens the door for chaos and punishment.

I want to end this chapter making you think. Are there any areas in our life, big or small, that we are compromising in? Are we complacent at times? Are we giving our entire lives to Christ? Or just parts? What is stopping us from growing? What is slowing us down or making us lose momentum? We have to be on constant watch, making sure we never allow a place for compromise. Nick Cruz, a former leader of a New York gang, now a Christian preacher and author, said this, "*We stink more of the world than we stink of sack cloth and Ashes. A lot of Contemporary Churches today would feel more at home in a Movie House rather than in a House of Prayer, more afraid of holy living than of sinning, know more about money than magnifying Christ in our bodies. It is so compromised that holiness and living a sin-free life is heresy to the modern Church.*"

"If SINNERS will be DAMNED, at least let them LEAP to HELL over our BODIES, and if they PERISH, let them PERISH with our ARMS around their KNEES imploring them to STAY. If HELL must be FILLED, at least let it be filled in the teeth of our EXERTIONS, and let NO ONE go there UNWARNED or UNPRAYED for." –Charles Spurgeon

"The fire doesn't make you what you are; it reveals what you were." -Jack Hyles

EIGHT

REVIVAL AND THE COST

Intro

This chapter has a little different meaning behind it than breaking tradition. I guess if I were to talk about the traditions related to revival, it's this: revival is for anyone hungry enough to run after God with everything they have. If you have read my first book I talk about a generation of workers who desire a large paycheck for minimal work. As we look around at our workforce, the turnover rate for jobs that require physical labor are ridiculous, mainly because they want the pay, but they don't desire to actually earn it. Revival can be the same way. We want a move of God but sometimes we are not willing to pay the price. We want our families saved and we want our marriage fixed, we want out of debt and we want to see ourselves healed and delivered, but we are not willing to sacrifice our compromise and complacency.

Here is the theme of this chapter: Do you really want it? Then run after it. Then hunger for it. Then do whatever it takes to take hold of it. One day you are going to look back on your life and give a testimony, what do you want your testimony to sound like? Will they read about you in the history books? Will what you build in this life survive the fire, or will it burn up (**1 Corinthians 3**)?

Revival history

Revival... we have all heard preachers talk about it. It's one of those things we want but sometimes we really don't understand it or why we need it. Throughout history revivals seemed so sporadic, from the number of American awakenings around the years 1727, 1792,1830, and 1882, to the Welsh Revival from 1904-1905, to the Azusa Revival in 1906, and even the Jesus movement in the 70's, these are just a small number of revivals in history. We tend to look at these and think that it's only for certain people, but in all honesty, I believe that revival can come to any nation, any city, any church, and any ministry. What was so special about these places and these people? What set these people apart? They were sold-out for God. They were hungry for the things of the Father. Most importantly of all, they knew the cost and were willing to die for it. At first when God told me to study the history or revival, I wasn't sure what the benefit of this study would be. I was always told to not live off of the things of the past. God spoke to me and said, "***Yes, you are not to live off the past revivals, but you can use them to fuel the revivals of today and tomorrow.***" In other words, we can take some of the knowledge from the past, combine it with the Holy Spirit, and watch God do a new thing within our community.

E.M. Bounds puts it like this, "*To look back upon the progress of the divine kingdom upon earth is to review revival periods which have come like refreshing showers upon dry and thirsty ground, making the desert to blossom as the rose, and bringing new eras of spiritual life and activity just when the Church had fallen under the influence of the apathy of the times.*"

Out of all the revivals I have read about so far there was one that really stuck out to me, and that is Zinzendorf and the Moravians. I know, the name is weird, but the history of this revival, I pray, will spark a passion in you that will make you examine your devotion to Christ. More than that, I desire for us to count the cost of living for Christ.

The Count and the Moravians

Count Nikolas Ludwig Von Zinzendorf was a man born of nobility in Dresden, Germany. He was saved at the age of 6 and at such a young age had a passion for God writing, "*I firmly resolved to live for Him alone who had laid down His life for me,*" and at the age of 9 he wrote, "*I have one passion, it's Jesus and Jesus only.*" Throughout his young life, Zinzendorf had a hunger for God that could not be quenched. (To read more about Zinzendorf and his history, I suggest you read a book called, "*Fire on the Altar,*" by Frank De Pietro.)

The year was 1722 and Nikolas and his wife had settled down on an estate they had just purchased. They both had given up their right of nobility to enter in the serving the Lord whole-heartedly. Before long, there was a knock on their door, it wasa man by the name of Christian David, a Moravian refugee. David was hoping that Zinzendorf could shelter him and some Moravian refugees on his land. At this time, Christians were being persecuted arcos the border into Moravia. Many were looking for the rebirth of a true New Testament Church, one that represented the church of Acts. They desired more, deeper things of God. Much like the Moravians, Christian David was a Catholic who could find no spiritual satisfaction within the catholic teachings, so he began his search for more. Ten times David crossed the borders into Moravia, bringing back refugee after refugee. The small group now totaled 300!

The group was filled with Lutherans, Calvinists, Catholics, Baptists, Separatists, and even Reformed, all looking for something more than what they had. Zinzendorf had one vision: To see a group of people who loved and supported one another through prayer, encouragement, and accountability. They named their small community, "*Herrnhut,*" meaning, "*The Lord's Watch.*" But of course, having many Christians with many different views had its challenges. There were quarrels, debates, division, and even men trying to lead others astray. For five years this went on. Eventually, over time, they began to see eye to eye as Zinzendorf taught them straight from the Bible.

In 1727 the group finally reached one accord and complete unity. They were truly an **Acts 2:4** church, "*Now all who believed were together, and had all things in common.*"

The power and glory of God hit that place hard. They began to have three services a day, which would always end the same way, weeping, deep repentance, and lying on the floor. Some refused to sleep because they were afraid to miss a move of God! There was even a moment when people who were working miles and miles away felt the glory of God so heavily. Revival was here!

Herrnhut lived by three scriptures, **1 Peter 1:16**, *"Be holy, for I am holy,"* **1 John 3:3**, *"Be pure, as Jesus is pure,"* and **Matthew 5:48**, *"Be perfect as your father in heaven is perfect."* Now, I understand that when we look at these scriptures we think impossible. But 1) they are scripture, which means they are TRUTH, and 2) when we hear the word, *"perfection,"* we tend to think that means we are without sin, but I believe God sees perfection differently. David was definitely not without sin, he fell many times throughout his life, but when it came down to it God called him a man after His own heart. I believe God isn't calling us to be without sin or fault, but He is looking to see if our hearts are completely towards Him no matter what. The Moravians believed that this was a lifestyle God had called them to pursue and strive for, and Jesus would not command something we could not achieve. What God's truth demands, His grace will surely provide for us, right? I think if we truly want revival we have to renew our mindset and see purity, holiness, and completeness an achievable goal through the Holy Spirit.

As the Revival continued to burn, they soon realized that as long as they kept their focus on Jesus, the Glory continued to prevail and overwhelm, but as soon as they would start to look at the work of each other or even begin to focus more on their work for God, the Glory would start to depart. They knew that if they wanted revival to stay they had to fuel the fire with prayer. Prayer was the catalyst that would fuel the revival fire. The Lord gave Zinzendorf a scripture, **Leviticus 6:13**, *"A fire shall always be burning on the altar; it shall never go out."* This scripture is what thrusted the Moravians into a 100-year intercessory prayer vigil. That's right, on August 27th twenty-four men and twenty-four women declared they would spend one hour each day in scheduled prayer. For twenty-four hours a day, seven days a week, from 1727 to 1827, they remained in prayer.

If you cannot tell already, the fire and passion these people had were absolutely amazing. It's hard to really see ourselves in that position because, I don't know about you, but I have a hard time staying in prayer for twenty minutes, let alone an hour a day for 100 years! The power they were moving in reminds me of Pentecost, and for some of us we never really think that the day of Pentecost could be repeated, but I believe it can. D.L. Moody writes, *"See how He came on the day of Pentecost! It is not carnal to pray that He may come again and that the place may be shaken. I believe Pentecost was but a specimen day. I think the church has made this woeful mistake that Pentecost was a miracle never to be repeated. I believe now if we looked upon Pentecost as a specimen day and began to pray, we should have the old Pentecostal fire here in Boston."* When will our prayers expand past the realm of possible and into the impossible? When will we get out of our comfort zone and step out for the world's sake? I believe in order to obtain revival we must believe for the impossible. We must pray bold prayers and truly believe them. These Moravians were just crazy enough to believe that God could take their village of 300 refugees and change the entire world! Even the disciples and the first church, "...Turned the world upside down (**Acts 17:6**)..." James Stewart writes, "*Revival is the people of God living in the power of an ungrieved, unquenched Spirit.*" Revival is waiting for a group of believers who desire God more than anything, to push aside their comfort zones and let the Spirit move freely.

This group of people was astonishing. Their passion was unmatched. They did more mission work in twenty years than the entire Church did in two centuries! Some even selling themselves into slavery in order to preach the gospel to slaves. Yet, we can't even talk to our coworkers.

In 1993, Jim Goll, former dean of the School of the Spirit at Grace Training Center in Kansas City, led a group of 19 Christians on a mission to Herrnhut. Their mission was to cross the border into Saxony, Germany to recover the anointing of the Moravian prayer watch. On occasion, visitors would be allowed to go up into the watchtower where the Moravians prayed. As they crossed the cemetery where the Moravians were buried, they made their way into the tower, up the stair case, and into the room where they prayed. As they stood in a circle they could feel the heaviness of God on them, and they all felt such a burden to cry out. They couldn't help but to pray and intercede.

The presence of God was so thick. One of the people wrote, "*...the best way I know how to say it is that I felt His grief and His longing for something Holy and powerful to be released... a feeling from His heart to my heart.*"

This group of hungry men and women of God would go on to spark awakenings and revivals all over the world in the centuries to come. There is so much more to these people, so many more stories, but I wanted to tell you this because I want to spark a fire within in you that says, "*I want more. I don't know what it is, but I want more of God.*" Revival is not something to be taken lightly. Maybe you are in revival now, I can't tell you how long it will last, but I can tell you one thing, grab onto it and run with it. As I have been reading about the great revivals all over the world, I began to see the same passions within my church and our people. It excited me, but also gave me a sense of responsibility. I do not want to waste my time. I do not want to take this for granted. But most importantly of all, I want to count the cost. Am I willing to give it all for God? Am I willing to forsake everything to experience an awakening?

Count the cost

I had woken up early one morning and headed to my backyard to sit and read. We have this old patio table we had bought at a moving sale, still dirty from the buy. As I sat down I had seen where my wife wrote in the dust and dirt, "*Count the cost.*" I could feel my heart stirring. Count the cost... one of those scriptures we tend to overlook or undervalue. **Luke 14:25-35** explains that a wise person does not start a project or go to war unless they first measure the cost or count their troops. Christianity is a beautiful life, but Jesus is saying that, although he desires all to be saved, we all must count the cost and understand that there will be things we will have to sacrifice. We must all weigh our faith and find out if it is truly worth it to us. Personally, from someone who has seen and experienced a lot with Christ, it's not always easy, but it's always worth it. The thing is, it took me a while to get to a place where I would truly lay my life down for God and those around me. I came to the conclusion that it's worth it all.

The sad truth is this: We have a generation of Christianity that isn't costing anyone anything. We have bought into a lie that we can have the fullness of Christ without sacrificing anything. It's easy in America to have a plan B, a plan C, even a plan D at times in our walk. God is calling us to burn the bridges behind us and have one plan: Jesus and only Jesus. When Elijah called upon Elisha to follow him, Elisha slaughtered his oxen and burnt his plow, making it so that he couldn't go back to his old life. God is calling us to do the same, not that God is saying we have to quit our jobs and burn our house down, but He is calling us to give him everything. Through Elisha's decision to follow the call, God is showing us that following Him is something not to be taken lightly.

I remember while at the event, Azusa Now, I felt God calling me to give financially to a certain ministry. My wife and I literally had $100 to our name. I began to make a deal with God, *"$20, Lord?"* He replied, *"More."* *"Ok, $40, Lord."* God replied again, *"More."* I was nervous right now and tried pretending that I didn't hear God. *"$60?"* Once again God replied, *"You know how much I want you to give."* My heart sank. I knew He wanted the whole $100, but I was nervous. I tried more than ever to offer $80 while still holding back the $20 as a back-up plan, but I knew what God wanted me to do. I gave our last $100 that day, but something broke in me in that moment. I officially didn't have a financial back-up plan. I had to completely trust in God, but in doing so, I broke open another level of faith in my life and God began to bring overflow into our lives. I will never forget that fear I felt debating with God, but once I did it, I felt a freedom like no other. Four years later and I still feel the influence that moment had on my life. To many, this may not seem like a big deal, but for me it was monumental. I had burned a bridge at that moment in my life.

God is calling you to burn the bridges of your back-up plans. There can be no fallback plans in case, *"God doesn't work out."* We have to trust that God's ways are far greater than anything we can think of or imagine. Yes, you will have to sacrifice things, you will have to give up friends, you will get persecuted, but God will restore those things and bring better into your life. I lost friends and I lost a girl I thought was, "the one," and I even had to give up jobs, but God has given me an amazing wife, the best friends and family I could imagine, and I have been blessed with so many amazing jobs. I counted the cost and I found it completely worth it.

Gather or filter?

The more I study the gospels the more I realize how different Jesus' ministry was compared to how so many of us do ministry here in America. Jesus had this crazy ability to gather large crowds but then preach these intense messages that filtered out those who truly wanted God and those who were just in it for the miracles. One of my favorite stories was when Jesus had thousands gathered before him and preached the, what I like to call, *"The Zombie Message,"* in **Luke 6**. Jesus begins to teach the crowd and says, *"I tell you the truth, unless you eat the flesh of the Son of Man and drink His blood, you have no life in you* (**Verse 53**).*"* Many of his disciples turned back and no longer followed him. Literally everybody except his twelve disciples left. Jesus turned to them and asked if they were going to leave too. Their response was amazing, *"Lord, to whom shall we go? You have the words of eternal life. We believe and know that you are the Holy One of God* (**verse 68**).*"*

Obviously, we know Jesus wasn't talking about actually eating his flesh and drinking his blood. This is why I call it the Zombie Message. Jesus was talking about spiritually consuming him and being "one" with Him. Any other ministry in America would devise a plan to keep every single one of those people gathered. We would have tried to entertain them, we would have put on events, established programs, brought out the beanbag chairs and the candy to get them to stay, and although those things are not bad, Jesus had a different mission than to just gather people, His goal was to show people that there is a cost to following Him. He loved them and He cared for their souls, but God isn't looking for a people who are kind of for Him, or sometimes for Him. He is looking for a people who are 100%, sold-out for Him and His kingdom!

I will ask you again like I asked in previous chapters; what is the point of having a packed church full of people, but they have no relationship with the Father? What's the point of having hundreds of tithers, yet none of them have truly encountered Jesus? What's the point of having a mega-church, but all of them being spiritually dead? I am not satisfied with filled churches. I hunger for more than just attendance. I hunger for revival. I hunger for people encountering God and being transformed into His image! I am persuaded that many leaders in the church talk of an unknown God and an unfelt Christ, and the reason that many churches are dead is because they have dead men and women leading them—men and women who either tried but settled because pressing in was too hard, or never even tried at all.

Many of us want to preach a message that will get people to get in the Church, but Jesus preached a message that challenged people to go out and BE the Church. We have too many Christians who want revival, they want the fullness of God, but are not willing to give it all to Him! The church is plagued with Lukewarm, casual Christianity and it's due to so many preachers preaching a gospel without cost. When I asked our roommate, Kelsie, a nurse, what revival meant to her, she said she thinks of a heart being shocked back to life. When a heart is shocked, it's current rhythm, if it has a rhythm, is disrupted in order to give it back it's healthy beat. It is literally jump started, and if you know anyone who has come back after a heart attack, they come back with a different perspective, with a fresh revelation of the importance of truly living. That's what I believe revival is, to literally be shocked back from death to life with a new perspective of why we are here.

I asked my wife the same thing and she was reminded of **Matthew 13** where the man found a treasure and went and sold everything he had in order to buy the field the treasure was in. When we know something is truly worth it, we will do whatever it takes to obtain it. We have to understand that relationship with God—His presence—is so amazing and beautiful that in order to obtain a deep, intimate relationship with Him, we must be willing to sell or give up everything we know and possess. So let me ask you again, is it really worth it to you? We have so many passions in this life, where we spend great amounts of money to get things, and we sacrifice so much of our time to achieve goals, and even strive with all our effort to get and build our lives, yet when it comes to the Creator, the one who died for you even when we were enemies, we tend to give him our leftovers, hoping our leftover time, money, and effort is enough for us to know God and experience revival.

William Booth once said, "*The chief dangers which confront the coming century will be religion without the Holy Ghost, Christianity without Christ, forgiveness without repentance, salvation without regeneration, politics without God, and heaven without hell."* My biggest concern is not that our amazing revival will cease to exist or someday die out, my biggest concern is that our people, and the body of Christ, will become content to live life without the fire, the love, the excitement, and the power of God. It saddens me when I see people trying to do Christianity without relationship. Yet, every Sunday thousands of preachers get up and preach about how much God loves us, and how He accepts us, and about all the blessings of God, but never once challenge believers to count the cost.

"Revival awakens in our hearts an increased awareness of the presence of God, a new hatred for sin, and a hunger for His Word." –Del Fehsenfeld Jr.

"The first step is a deep repentance, a breaking down of heart, a getting down into the dust before God, with deep humility, and a forsaking of sin." –Charles Finney

"The only reason we don't have revival is because we are willing to live without it." Leonard Ravenhill

"If you are a stranger to prayer, then you will be a stranger to revival." –C.J. Greiner

"You never have to advertise a fire. Everyone comes running when there's a fire. Likewise, if your church is on fire, you will not have to advertise it. The community will already know it." - Leonard Ravenhill

"If my people, who are called by my name, shall humble themselves, and pray, and seek my face, and turn from their wicked ways; then will I hear from heaven, and will forgive their sin, and will heal their land." **2 Chronicles 7:14**

FINAL WORDS

This book has been such a crazy journey. Some of you may be overwhelmed by it all. Maybe you're asking, "*Why are you so adamant about all of this?*" It's because I hit my head. Yes, I hit my head. One day I was at work in my warehouse when I had to squeeze between two stacks of pallets. I got what I needed and as I turned around and begin to lift my head I hit my head on the corner of a pallet. For those who don't know I don't really have any hair on the top of my head to protect me from anything. I skinned my head very badly and man was I mad. In my moment of anger, the Lord spoke to me, "***Pay attention.***" "*Seriously? That's the advice I get?*" I laugh at the whole situation now but, in that moment, I was confused and my head was bleeding. God spoke again, "***Many of my people are like you in this moment. They are walking around in this life with their heads down, doing this and doing that, believing whatever makes them feel good, and when the enemy comes and strikes them and knocks them down, they are somehow surprised. My people are lost and unaware that they are, and in their confusion, the enemy is knocking them back and forth, and they are surprised by it all.***"

As I have said before, there is no hit like the one you don't see coming. That is the hit that really knocks you down. When you are not prepared or you are not taught correctly, you will fail and you will get hurt, and in your pain you will begin to sculpt an idea of God's nature based out of your emotions and your own failures. And that is why God called me to write this book, to turn the hearts of His people back to their first love: God. I want to see the Body of Christ prosper the way it was created to. I want to see families restored, children growing, and churches thriving just like the ministry of Christ. I want to see prayers answered and passion ignited. It so easy to believe and jump on board any doctrine that sounds good and makes you feel good, but my goal is that we mature, learn God's voice, and cultivate wisdom and discernment through relationship with the Father, so that we can know what is of God and what is not.

When there is a spirit of confusion or deception in our land, in our churches, and in our hearts, that is when we are in dire need of revival, but not just as a whole, we need a personal revival in our lives. Our hearts must spark and ignite. We must get to a point where there is a renewed conviction of sin and repentance, followed by a deep desire to live for God with full obedience. Whether you believe you live for Him fully now or not, our desire to live for God should always be increasing, and we do that by relationship. There can be no true prosperity in our lives when confusion and deception prevails.

I pray you have been blessed by this book, even if it was just one section that really spoke to you. It's time we rise up and step into the life that God is calling us to live. It's time we die to the traditions of men and come to life in the power of God.

You can also check out C.J. Greiner's first book, *#DearChristianMen*, for sale on **Amazon.com** or **CreateSpace.com**

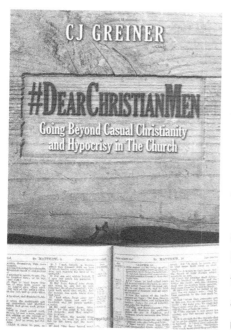

Are you a man struggling to find your purpose within God's kingdom? Is Christianity just a Sunday morning activity with no life or energy? Do you long to experience the real love of God?

#DearChristianMen is a book by a Christian man for Christian men. It is an impassioned plea for men (and women) to move away from a casual Christian lifestyle into a compelling, vibrant faith that leads by example. Filled with chapters on difficult topics such as becoming a man of God, fighting lust and pornography, and understanding God's love for us, author C.J. Greiner offers a bold, transparent, and ultimately inspiring book that will both challenge and motivate.

For Christians of any age, this engaging work pulls directly from scripture to encourage men to commit their lives completely to God.

Made in the USA
Columbia, SC
25 March 2019